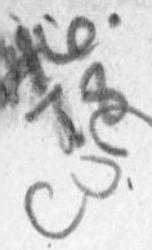

★ HOW TO WIN A ★

FAMILY FIGHT

WILL CUNNINGHAM

Multnomah® Publishers *Sisters, Oregon*

HOW TO WIN A FAMILY FIGHT
published by Multnomah Publishers, Inc.

International Standard Book Number: 1-59052-644-9

Cover design by The DesignWorks Group, Inc.

Printed in the United States of America

With permission, all entries have been edited for publication, and names and some other specifics have been changed for various reasons.

For information:
MULTNOMAH PUBLISHERS, INC. • 601 N LARCH STREET • SISTERS, OR 97759

Library of Congress Cataloging-in-Publication Data
Cunningham, Will, 1959-
How to win a family fight / by Will Cunningham.
p. cm.
Rev. ed. of: How to enjoy a family fight. c1988.
ISBN 1-59052-644-9
1. Family—United States—Psychological aspects. 2. Interpersonal conflict—United States. 3. Communication in the family—United States. I. Cunningham, Will, 1959- How to enjoy a family fight. II. Title.
HQ734.C96 2006
646.7'8—dc22
2006008114

06 07 08 09 10—10 9 8 7 6 5 4 3 2

Dedication

To Jean, my mom…for everything.

In Latin, she is "mater."
In French, she is the "mere."
In Greek, she is a "meter"…
Measuring stick of kindred cheer.
In German, she's the "mutter."
In Russian, she's the "mat."
But in my heart, she's just my "mom."
And I'm okay with that.

(Written for Jean Cunningham twenty Mother's Days ago.)

Will's Disclaimer

It is important for me to mention somewhere before we get started that some of the names in this book are made-up names—straight out of my head, like the characters in a story one tells around a fire. I have withheld the authentic names mostly to avoid being sued, but also because I love the characters I've met in the pages of this story I've come to know as My Life.

However, just because the names are fabricated doesn't make my stories any less real or substantial than if I were to, say, exclaim to you one suppertime that I was so hungry I could eat a horse. Of course you would recognize the exaggeration, but you would never in a million years call me a liar. You've known that same kind of "horse hunger" in your own life. My desire is to create in you now a new kind of "God hunger." If I have to tell a stretcher or two to have my way, then God forgive me.

What I'm trying to say here is that everything in this book happened exactly as I've said it did, with only a few embellishments, five or twelve augmentations, and the occasional adjustment of facts. Besides that, it's all true.

As far as you know.

Contents

Acknowledgments

Every five years or so I dream about going to school in just my underwear. They tell me this is a universal phenomenon. But I don't care how many people in the universe are doing it; I expect my subconscious to get the heck dressed and stay that way.

In real life I always remember to show up for the important events with my clothes on. So you would think the same forethought would carry to all areas of my life. Occasionally, however, I slip up and am reminded why I was never a Boy Scout: I am as prepared for life as a snowman in July.

Once I was traveling with my family to speak at a youth retreat in the mountains of central Colorado. Suddenly my Neanderthal brain registered that I had no notes, no outline, and nothing to say. This was not because I had left my work at home. It was because I really had nothing to say.

"What should I do?" I asked my family.

"Drive real fast, and then jump out of the car," said Wesley from the backseat.

"Throw up," said Peter.

"Call Doug," said Cindy, handing me her phone. She had already dialed the number. It rang four times before the voice of my mountain buddy came through the lines—like chocolate on fiber optics.

For several minutes he listened to my predicament. "What should I do?" I asked.

His answer pierced my slothfulness. "Tell stories, talk about Jesus, and be appropriately vulnerable."

"That's it?"

"Yep—works every time."

"Thanks. You're the smartest man in the universe."

When we hung up, I felt a burden had been lifted from my miserable, procrastinating carcass. I tested Doug's advice, and to my delight the weekend was as enjoyable as any speaking engagement I have ever participated in.

Since then, I've decided that ready or not, Doug's patented "stories, Jesus, and vulnerability" approach simply can't be beat. Plagiarism has made it mine over time, which is why nineteen years after *Family Fight* was first published, readers of the initial edition will notice a greater emphasis on entertainment, discipleship, and self-deprecating stories the second time around.

I've had a lot of fun writing the new edition, which is what I set out to do. But I also hope *you* have fun, and that you get to know me in the following chapters. After all, what finer remedy is there in life than laughter in the midst of pain, and a good friend or two with whom to share it? This is one of the secrets to winning a family fight.

As for vulnerability, I have been as honest as I can without embarrassing my wife, alerting the authorities to my whereabouts, or painting such a weirdsmobile picture of myself that you might wonder whether you are in good hands. As a professional marriage counselor, I assure you I know my topic well...very well. I simply don't want to be viewed as a know-it-all, or as one who flawlessly obeys the things he writes about.

As to the business of thanking people:

Cindy—you come first. Thank you for loving the real me, while having pity on the wretched one. When Christ who is my life appears, I too will appear with Him in glory, and then you'll see it was not such a bad idea to say "I do" back in 1982. You're the best.

Wes and Pete, you've both beaten me at chess and H-O-R-S-E, and are almost able to take me on the mat, so this is as good a time as any to throw in the towel. My dynasty is over. Thanks for becoming men. God's kingdom is rarely led by boys.

Thanks also to the noble kin who came before me—to Mom, to Harvey, to Dodo. From you I received a love for God, for people, and for the English language.

Finally, Dad, I would thank you, too, if you hadn't left the party so early. True to form, you bolted from one more thing that hurt you in life. But, by golly, while you were still alive, you always stood like steel against the things that hurt the Savior. I look forward to playing catch with you in heaven. I'll bet you have a wicked curveball by now. Anyway, I hope I recognize you with your new hair. I'll be the guy in his underwear.

As for you, the reader, let's go learn to fight—while there's still breath in us.

Will Cunningham

Introduction

THE THINGS I'D HAVE SAID

If I had an older man's wisdom
when I wore a younger man's clothes,
these are the things I'd have said.

Steinbeck once said he was sorry for losing touch with the nation about which he wrote so beautifully. To make up for it, he and his poodle circled the United States in a rattletrap truck named Rocinante and recorded it all in a book called *Travels with Charley.*

I am not famous like John Steinbeck, but I know how it feels to lose touch with one's material. When I wrote the first edition of *How to Enjoy a Family Fight* in 1987, I believed there was nothing more urgent than teaching people an effective approach to conflict. But eventually I moved on to other projects, and my own words faded out like a song that has fallen from the charts. It wasn't until my job required me to travel across the South during the late nineties that the tune came back to me—and I remembered it word for word.

"Who ya fer?" snapped the gas station attendant in Birmingham, as I handed him my bag of chips and a Coke. He punched their cost into the register and glared at me through a sweaty crop of familiar eyebrows. I had passed a Mississippi kite an hour or so west of there, perched on a wire, eyeing a dead rabbit in the ditch, and for the life of me this fellow seemed just as hungry for my answer as that bird did for its breakfast.

"Who ya fer?" he repeated.

Who was I *fer*? I had no idea who I was *fer*, because I had no idea what he was asking.

"What do you mean, exactly…sir?"

"Tigers or Tide, boy. Are ya igner'nt?"

"No, sir, I'm not igner'nt."

"Then, who ya fer?"

"I, uh…"

"You ain't from around here, are ya?"

"I'm from Oklahoma," I said, just glad to answer a question. "You know…the Sooner state? Actually, I'm not a Sooner. I went to Oklahoma State, so technically that makes me a Cowboy. But I like the Sooners."

Suddenly, Who-Ya-Fer was no longer interested in my pedigree. "Drink and chips come to a buck ninety-two," he said coldly.

I paid him and had started toward the door when his next words lassoed me and pulled me back.

"My second wife was an Auburn Tiger."

"That's…nice."

The man glared at me. "Nothin' nice about it, boy. She made my life right miserable."

"I'm sorry."

"No need to feel sorry, boy. She left me after the '75 homecoming."

I spouted the first condolence that came to mind. "That must have been an awful time for you."

"It was the best thing that ever happened to me."

"Right. Okay." *Something positive.* "Well, see you on down the road."

I headed again toward the door, but Who-Ya-Fer wasn't ready to let me go. He reached for something beneath the counter and I froze, visualizing the next day's headline:

STATION ATTENDANT UNLEASHES YEARS OF TWELVE-GAUGE FRUSTRATION ON UNSUSPECTING CUSTOMER

"I might have kept her if she was a Cowboy," he offered, pulling a cigarette lighter from the shelf beneath the register. He winked at me as he lit his cigarette.

"Thank you," I blurted, then added, "and the Big Twelve thanks you, too."

Who-Ya-Fer laughed out loud, and for the first time I noticed he had a tiny elephant tattooed on his right cheek. "Right on," he said, and the elephant did a little dance. "Roll Tide."

"Oh, yeah. Definitely. Roll Tide. Roll all the way to the National Championships. Am I right? Am I talking? Ha ha. Okey-dokey, I'm out of here."

"Want yer chips, Cowboy?"

"Nope—not really hungry anymore."

A mile down the highway I realized I had also left my Coke on the counter. I swallowed dryly, punched the gas, and rolled as fast as I could toward Atlanta.

It was like that all the way across the great planet of Alabama. In every small town I was asked, "Tigers or Tide, boy? Auburn or Alabama?" I soon realized a great many folks wouldn't even pass the cheese grits until I swore my allegiance one way or the other.

What I'm trying to say is that you haven't wasted your money buying this book. Just as Auburn and Alabama need some rules to survive their annual clash on the gridiron, so people need rules to survive marital conflict, boardroom conflict, relational conflict, or any other kind of conflict.

After polling hundreds of serious-minded Southerners, I have determined that Auburn and Alabama football players have a better chance of escaping unscathed from a game of football than do the unfortunate spouses who choose opposite sides in the Tiger-Tide rivalry.

Almost two decades have passed since my wife and I first developed the curriculum for applying sports rules to conflict resolution.

The first class was an instant hit, complete with referee shirts, whistles, video clips of soap opera–style fighting, and flags for people to throw whenever rules of good conflict were violated. Some of our original students are still unable to watch *Monday Night Football* without recalling discussion on chapters like "Offsides," "Too Many Players on the Field," and "Backfield in Motion."

Most of my original concepts are still relevant today. But the language in which I first communicated them had to go through a bit of a makeover. For the most part, however, all of the rules for a good fight remain intact.

Cindy and I still believe marital conflicts in the new millennium are like athletic events: There are always two opponents, both want to win, and most family fights happen on weekends—usually Sunday.

Nevertheless, I am a different person today. And I approach conflict resolution with a new and different set of beliefs.

So what is it about the topic of fighting that still captivates me after all this time?

It does seem odd, doesn't it, that a Christian author would keep focusing on something so negative. Maybe it's because humans are maddeningly squeamish about admitting conflict is part of the fabric of our relationships. We stiff-arm the subject, tolerating its appearance in others but never in ourselves.

Yet fighting is all around us. Attorneys study for years to be adversarial. Doctors arm themselves with knowledge to wage war against deadly diseases. Farmers fight weeds. Firemen fight fires. Computer technicians fight the viruses that invade our homes and offices. Athletes train for battle so the rest of us can be entertained.

With such a wartime mentality pervading society, it is a mystery why thousands of brides and grooms continue skipping down aisles—as though they are tripping off to garden parties, where doting waiters will offer delicacies on silver trays for the next fifty years.

I tell you, someone ought to ride a horse through the center of every wedding ceremony, shouting, "The redcoats are coming! The redcoats are coming!" And they would be telling the truth. For every Mr. and Mrs. Giddy who drive away from a church parking lot in a rented limo, a legion of red devils pour from hell, hot on their trail.

How tragically unprepared for warfare we are—especially Christians.

Disharmony is no respecter of religions. Given today's odds, I would just as soon bet the house on a Hindu marriage as one consummated under the sign of the cross. Blasphemy? One glance at the marriage obituaries in any newspaper acquits me of the charge.

Deist, theist, or me-ist, everyone who dons a wedding ring must make an important decision: Will I subject myself to a body of rules that allows me to live peacefully with another fallen being? Or will I fool myself into believing my fabric is somehow less shabby than the rest of humanity's?

We are all cut from the same cloth. In twelve years of professional marriage counseling and twenty-seven years of Christian ministry I have seen both heathen and holy men abuse their wives with equal proficiency. I have known candidates for The Most Difficult Woman to Live With award who represent all three of the world's monotheistic religions. And I have witnessed shocking divorces in the ranks of my own ministry colleagues.

Is it likely that anyone escapes our universal tendency toward relationship homicide? Not remotely. We blow away loved ones with the coolness of a serial killer. We not only eat our young; we butter their heads and pin their ears before the first bite. We are barbarians in church clothes, badly in need of someone to set us straight.

Isaiah said it well when he wrote, "Everyone has gone astray, each to his own way." Logic follows that if I habitually choose my way, then by default I habitually reject your way, and God's as well…which makes for a lot of unhappiness all around.

In the following pages I am going to tell stories, talk about Jesus, and be so vulnerable with you that before you are halfway done with this book, your family fights will already feel more positive…and godly even. My stories will focus on rules from sports (football, basketball, golf, bowling, etc.), and will show how these rules must be followed in order for each player in a family fight to feel like a winner.

But this is not a book about sports.

This is a book about God and the biblical truths written to help relationships hold together; that's why many chapters are followed by short segments filled with spiritual reflection. The sports twist is there merely to help you remember things—sort of like the ESPN jingle at the beginning of the broadcast.

DA-DA-DA!!

DA-DA-DA!!

You are no more likely to forget the truths in this book than you are to forget the ESPN jingle. They are designed to touch the wretched competitive nature in you—the one that says, "I must beat my opponent at all costs." The one that God is dying to put to death.

Here is something for you to hang on to: God is truly for you. The important question is…who are *you* fer? Are you so *fer* your relationships, *fer* your wife, *fer* your husband, *fer* your children, and *fer* your friends that you are willing to learn and be governed by a whole new set of conflict resolution rules?

If your answer is yes, then you are ready for the next step toward winning a family fight.

Roll on.

Digging to China

THE GIFT OF PAIN

It's not hard to stay married—all you have to do is open up an artery and bleed.

No sweeter kisses exist on earth than those of my wife and only pucker-partner until death do us part. But Cindy was not the first person I ever kissed, and if I were able to murder the memory of this one endearment, I would wring its neck vigorously.

It was a cold night in Oklahoma City, and I had just wrecked my father's Buick. In my defense, I was trying to avoid a cat when I struck the patch of black ice, spun three times, demolished a mailbox, and wound up in the south ditch of the Northwest Expressway. The cat was grateful, I'm sure. My date, on the other hand, was not.

An hour later, after trudging through calf-high snow (this was before the invention of the cell phone), we reached her house, only to discover the front door, back door, side door, and every window locked tighter than Scrooge's miserly heart. Now

I'm no doctor, but I'm pretty sure when my date told me she couldn't feel her feet inside her moon boots that we had a problem on our hands.

"Do you have a woodpile?" I asked.

"Y-y-yes," she replied through jackhammering teeth.

"Where is it?"

"Be-be-behind the ga-ga-garage."

"Let's find some matches and get you warmed up a little."

After rifling through the measly twigs that comprised the "woodpile" and discovering a dry book of matches and some old rags in her father's tool chest, we started a fire in an empty birdbath.

My date eyed the anemic flames and stuck out a pouty lip.

"Do you have any lighter fluid?" I asked.

"There's a gasoline can next to the lawn mower."

"Perfect."

(This is a good place to insert the text "Will is an idiot.")

The explosion blew a hole in the hedge next to the birdbath. It was really very enchanting, what with the backyard lit up like the Fourth of July and my date bawling from the sheer horror of it all. Suddenly every lamp in the house came on and her dad started shouting from his bedroom window, "What the heck's going on out there?" (which was not really what he said, but it represents the spirit in which he addressed me).

"Just reenacting the Tet Offensive in your backyard, sir. Don't you love the smell of napalm in the morning? I hope so. Because it's, like…really early in the morning."

"What kind of nut are you?"

"Just the average kind."

Certain our time together was coming to an end, yet always the gentleman, I took my date's hand and gazed apologetically into her terrified eyes.

"Can I walk you to the door?"

"Please," she begged.

I navigated us both across the frozen lawn, tiptoeing carefully between smoldering leaves and twigs, until we finally reached the back porch. At the top stair, I turned and looked her in the eyes again.

"This has been nice."

"Yeah…really nice."

"Would you mind if I kissed you?"

For the briefest moment, my date's expression wavered between "Are you a moron?" and "Yes, I think I'd like to get this over with."

Oblivious to the context clues, I stepped closer, turned my head slightly, and placed what I believed was the kiss to end all kisses on the slightly blue lips of my nearly frozen date.

Everything would have been just fine, and I'm sure she would have leaped at the prospect of future dates, had I only left well enough alone. But to this day, I regret the next four words that fairly gushed forth.

"I love you, Jill," I said.

My date's corpselike face turned an angry shade of red. "The name's Lisa," she hissed. "Who is Jill?"

"Did I say Jill?"

"You said Jill."

"Well, what I meant to say was—*Will.* 'I love you, *Will'.* You see? 'I love you…*Willll.'* Okay? Like, if you think about it, if you look at it from just the right angle…what I was really saying…were the words *I* wanted *you* to say to me, Jill."

"Lisa."

"I mean Lisa."

"Get out of here."

"I'll be going now."

You would think I'd count my losses and slink away into the shadows. But Lisa's back porch possessed no handrail and was elevated six feet above her father's snow-encrusted marigolds. When I turned to make my exit, I landed with a thud in the flowerbed, where for a moment I considered burrowing with my teeth to China just so I wouldn't have to pick my God-forsaken carcass out of the snow and face Jill again, or Lisa, or whatever the heck her name was.

"I'm okay down here! Little cold. Lotta moisture. Good night. Call me." With that, I trudged off in search of my father's Buick.

Several months later I tried to reach Lisa/Jill by phone to see if she had forgiven me, and whether she wanted to enjoy another date, but the recording informed me her number had been changed and the new one was not available to the public.

People are so paranoid.

Undaunted by my early attempts at relating to the opposite sex, I eventually stumbled into love with a woman named Cindy, whose name means "goddess of the moon."

Cindy and I had been working together in a ministry to troubled teens. After months of trying to convince the moon goddess to go out with a mortal like me, I finally talked her into it.

It was 1981—an excellent year for love. We were driving north on Missouri Highway 65, surrounded by the markings of early December: Canada geese landing in Ford Field, fog hovering over Lake Taneycomo, smoke curling from chimneys and resting in the Ozark hollows.

Our destination was Springfield, where we planned to watch a group of high school boys play basketball. Afterwards we had reservations at a nice restaurant. It was our first real date, and I was not going to blow it by calling her the wrong name, or blowing up her father's birdbath, or…running into that pickup that was driving toward us—*in our lane!*

Cindy never saw it coming. She was looking down at her lap, reading a card I had made for her. I didn't have time to swerve. The sound of metal on metal woke the morning. Cindy's Honda bounced, spun, careened into the Bee Creek Bridge guardrail, ricocheted off, and finally came to a halt.

Like a marionette with cut strings, I felt limp. I tasted blood. Heard a crunch as I tried to move. Broken glass? Broken teeth? I licked my lips—split clean through from nose to chin, blessedly numb.

My mind registered several sights:

A steering wheel bent into a half-moon…

Missing windshield…

Tape deck…

Glove box…

Hand brake…

Hand—

A woman's hand.

I saw the torn card…

Ripped jeans, red and wet…

Bone…

White…

Jagged…

Legs twisted around the wrecked engine…

Hot and hissing into her lap.

Cindy turned and moaned, her broken hands clawing for help.

Sirens blared.

Men shouted orders.

Wind blew through the car, like the devil through a frozen whistle.

I shivered.

Closed my eyes.

Let my head fall back against the bloody seat.

**Life is like a bottle of Italian dressing—
never fully satisfying until well shaken.
(I just made that up.)**

Two weeks after the crash, on Christmas morning, after weeks of morphine, traction, splints, casts, surgeries, stitches, intravenous feeding, blood transfusions, armies of well-wishers, and tubes stuck in every available orifice...I felt it might be time to wake up.

Happy as hens to have a romantic diversion from their jobs, the nurses wheeled Cindy's and my hospital beds into the sunroom and peered from behind curtains to see what would happen next. Dawn, like an angel, came softly through the windows at the foot of our beds, and out over the valley we saw the highway meandering across the frozen floor of the Ozarks.

"My hands don't look so good, do they?" said Cindy, breaking the silence.

She was right. They were covered with thick purplish scar tissue from the lacerations she received when the windshield exploded in on us.

"I'll always hold your hand, Cindy," I answered. "You've just never given me the chance."

We both burst out laughing—I belly-laughed so hard that my hip, now secured with screws, felt on fire. But if this was courtship, I thought, give me more pain.

Cindy reached across the space between our beds and for the first time held my hand. "I love you, Will Cunningham."

"I love you, too, C."

A single, silver tear appeared in the corner of Cindy's eye, and we both had no idea what to say next. So we just sat there with tubes sticking out of us, Mr. and Mrs. Frankenstein holding hands and basking in the weirdness of it all. Eventually the nurses came out of hiding to wheel us back to our rooms, and that was the end of the basking.

It was also the beginning of real healing for our bodies, and the birth of true love for each other—a lifetime of love.

Looking back at our lives since December 5, 1981, I see two things: pain and gain.

There was the pain of loss. I lost the feeling in my entire left side as a result of the crash. Even now as I type, I'm often forced to watch the keys because I cannot feel them beneath my left hand. I also lost my ability to play the guitar and to participate in some of my favorite sports—things I have since relearned, but only after a long road back.

Cindy lost as much as I. Sixteen broken bones robbed her of beloved pastimes—jogging and racquetball. But never once have I heard her complain.

If we could relive the past and escape that pain, but it meant missing out on even a fraction of the gain—a strong, thriving marriage and two really cool sons—then Cindy and I would not cash in a single twinge.

★ ★ ★

Saint Augustine once said, "Better to have loved and lost, than to have never loved at all."

I think what the saint was trying to say was that true love—whether the ridiculous, puppy love kind, or the deep, decades-old kind—will always involve some kind of pain. His quote reminds me of something my high school football coach used to say: *No pain, no gain.*

It flies in the face of logic, doesn't it? Our bodies ache, our thoughts are in turmoil, our marriages and relationships are worn at the seams. Where's the good that justifies the pain?

Nonetheless, it's true. Even your relational conflicts can be a source of tremendous blessing, if you allow yourself to learn from them.

There *is* gain in pain.

Lisa/Jill's marigolds suggest it.

Bee Creek Bridge proves it.

All you have to do is believe it.

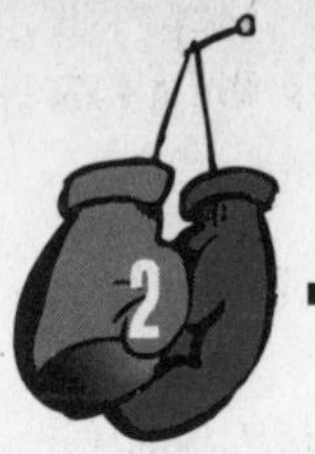

The Demigod's Left Drawer

OFFSIDES

I jumped offsides so many times in my high school football career, my coach started calling me—well, let's just say he wasn't happy.

Timing is everything when it comes to stand-up comedy and family fights. Oh, and it's probably a good idea to have a sense of timing with your taxes.

Our government has a great sense of timing, but a horrible sense of humor. I think they need to laugh more while they're counting the money up there at the old IRS building.

"All right, Gus—what does that bring us to today?"

"Five hundred and sixty billion, three hundred and forty-two million, seven hundred and fifty-three dollars and twenty-two cents."

"Hmm—seems a little light. Is it me, or are we missing something?"

"Well, here's this IOU from a Mr. William W. Cunningham for thirty-eight bucks in federal. He says he'll have it to us by

July, when he gets his birthday check from his mom."

"Whooop! That's a good one. That Mr. Cunningham sure is a funny individual. Ha ha ha! Oh gosh, I think I cracked a rib."

"Hee hee hee!"

"Ho ho!"

Wheeze

Cough

"Gus?"

"Hmmm?"

"Send Roberts to break Mr. Cunningham's legs."

"Got it."

"Good night."

"Good night."

Timing is everything when it comes to family fights.

I was an offensive tackle in high school, and I learned early on that timing was not my strong suit.

I blamed it on adrenaline.

"Coach, I can't help it if I'm offsides. I just want to beat someone…fire off the line…shiver my man in the chin with a powerful forearm!"

"That's beautiful, Cunningham. Why don't you go over there and prop your powerful forearms on the water cooler."

Come to think of it, I was more suited for tennis than football. Nevertheless, I lettered and kept playing, and wound up earning a lot of penalties during my high school career.

I also took it personally when the referee blew his whistle and called my number whenever I would jump across the line before the ball was snapped. I felt as if he were penalizing me for enthusiasm. But I know now that was not the case. It was my *timing* that cost my team so dearly.

When Cindy and I first developed these thoughts on conflict resolution, we knew we needed to start with timing. There is hardly a time when a person *has* to fight—as though, if he doesn't express his anger immediately, his spleen will explode. Nobody is in that big of a hurry to fight—at least, he shouldn't be.

My favorite book is *To Kill a Mockingbird*. It is a glorious train wreck of a book, the kind too big, too close, and too attractive to avert your eyes from. So you watch...and you weep.

Throughout *Mockingbird*, lawyer Atticus Finch dispenses wisdom. He is the one who draws the bead on the rabid dog and drops him in the road, the one white man who swears to his own hurt that God made black men his equal. Atticus Finch is the calm voice in the storm, and I want very much to be like him.

"It's not time to worry yet," he tells his kids in every situation. By the end of the book, it is still not yet time.

Just as it is not the time to worry in Atticus's world, it is usually not the time to get angry and fight. Oh, there are times when it is necessary, but they are few. I wish I could take back some of those occasions when I thought it was time to be angry and wound up jumping offsides with my family.

One time in particular stands out in my mind. Peter wasn't

even in school yet when this happened. The story has a funny element to it, but it is mostly sad. Sometimes when I think of it, I watch it unfold in my head…and I feel like weeping.

He was sitting on the garage steps that December evening when I came home from work, in his favorite place, doing his favorite thing—waiting for daddy.

"Hello, my pirate," I said to Peter. I closed the door to my Blazer, and he was in my arms.

"Did you miss me?"

"No."

★ ★ ★

I think it's impossible for really little children to miss someone. When we leave them they know we are coming back, eventually—like the face that reappears from behind cupped hands in a game of peek-a-boo. While the face is gone, life goes on merrily. And when the face returns, life becomes even merrier. I think kids inherently trust in the Second Coming, and would articulate it if they could do so. It is only we adults who fear our aloneness in the universe, and develop schemes like atheism to cope with it. Truth be known, we miss our Maker—and we pass this separation anxiety along to our children.

"So…you didn't miss me?" I asked again, fishing for love. I set Peter back down on the concrete, and he took me by the hand, yanking me toward the opposite side of the garage. "What is it, little man?"

At my workbench Peter opened the top left-hand drawer,

stood back, and smiled. Inside my normally ordered drawer (I should say, "compulsively ordered"), it looked like a small bomb had gone off. Bits of paper, hair, leaves, and food were so strewn that I couldn't even see the tools. I looked at Peter, who was gazing at me with satisfaction.

"Do you know who did this?" I asked suspiciously.

Peter smiled and nodded.

I became instantly stern.

"Young man, it looks like you have some undoing to do."

Peter's smile faded, as I metastasized from fun-guy to angry-guy right before his eyes. I piled the trash in his outstretched hands and kept on yipping at him as he went back and forth from trash can to drawer, making right what he had done, bringing order back to Daddy's drawer.

"It's not so cute and funny anymore, is it?" I asked.

Peter ignored my rhetoric and kept on cleaning, having been sanitized of whatever wonderment he had been waiting on his step, for who knows how long, to share with me. Eventually the drawer was restored, and we went in for dinner, where I pasted on a happy face for the rest of the family—but Peter hardly looked up from his plate.

The next day when I came home from work, there was Peter again. We went through the same ritual—the "hello, my pirate," the hug, the great, arcing swing up into the arms of a demigod. And then I noticed the look of caution on his face.

"What's the matter, pal?" I asked.

He was looking in the direction of the drawer.

"Peter?" I said, this time more forcefully. *"What* is the *matter?"*

I took him by the hand and led him over to the workbench, where I opened the drawer very slowly, prolonging my disappointment. Inside, my fears were verified.

"Peter!" I took him by the shoulders and pulled him closer

to the drawer so he could see the mess inside. "Do you know who's responsible for this?"

Peter looked at me and nodded again.

"All right—that's it! No supper for you tonight. You're going straight to bed! And maybe while you're lying there in the dark, you can figure out why you think it's okay to keep trashing my things."

After supper I went out and cleaned the drawer myself.

I do not know why parents withhold food as punishment. Maybe we believe that godly repentance results from hunger pains. But if this were true, why is it that God still blesses the crops of the Taliban, and sends rain on them, and waters their thirsty gullets? If I were God and I came home one evening to discover that someone had made a mess of my Trade Center, or knocked down my Twin Towers, you can bet I'd be shutting off someone's water pretty quickly. Heads would roll—turbaned heads.

Maybe that's why I'm not God.

Now, I align neatly with Ecclesiastes and with C. S. Lewis's views on war in his book *The Weight of Glory*. I believe there is a place for retaliation, and a time for the pacifist to understand that the law of love sometimes requires a man to defend a loved one by punishing a foe—or else he is less than an infidel.

All I'm trying to say here is that whatever drives the lineman to leap offsides is sometimes the same thing that causes a president to order a bombing, or a father to send his son to bed without supper.

Timing is everything, for with time comes the opportunity to gather the facts—at least more thoroughly than I did at my workbench with Peter.

★ ★ ★

The third day when I pulled into the garage, Peter was not on his favorite step. Who can blame him? I put my Blazer in park, turned off the engine, walked to the workbench, and opened the drawer.

Then I went to find Peter, so I could spank him.

Solomon was purportedly the wisest man who ever lived, with understanding "as measureless as the sand on the seashore" (1 Kings 4:29). He was a writer, a musician, a botanist, a zoologist, a statesman, a philosopher, and a king.

I do not doubt that he was wise, except when I read that he had seven hundred wives.

This has always perplexed me; it would appear that on a number of occasions the wisest man in the world slipped into a mild coma. Seven hundred wives—that's like two wives for every day of the year. I think all the sex in the world for Solomon couldn't make up for the lousy family fights he was sure to have.

"Honey, I'm serving lamb tonight for supper—what would you like to go with it?"

"Excuse me…but…what's your name?"

"Queen Zelda. What's it going to be, dear—leeks or onions?"

"Do we know each other?"

"Oh, for crying out loud, Solomon, fix your own supper."

Now, I am not trying to be irreverent; the Bible does a good job on its own of exposing the foolish sides of even its wisest men. But I've also got to wonder about all the kids that were surely the result of Solomon's many marriages.

The book of 1 Kings tells us that Solomon not only had Israelite wives, but Moabites, Ammonites, Edomites, Hittites, and Sidonians. The man had a wife in every port.

It stands to reason, then, that everywhere Solomon went he couldn't hide from his fatherly responsibilities. No wonder he coined such proverbs as "The fear of the LORD is the beginning of knowledge" and "He that spares the rod hates his son." I was having trouble enough handling Peter, let alone hundreds of sons just like him.

These and other thoughts were going through my head as I spanked my boy that night and slunk back across the house to the garage to clean my drawer for the third time.

It was a lonely evening.

I played a lot of sports, earned some letters, and have some ribbons to prove it; but I'm not really an athlete. Real athletes *have* to compete, or something deep inside of them snaps. For me, competition is like Earth Day—it comes, it goes, I'm hardly aware of its passing.

Families, on the other hand, I would die for.

This is the reason for all the talk about rules of conflict in this book. I am passionate about getting this message in your heart, then reminding you of it over and over and over—like every time you turn on ESPN.

Families are the ticket; sports are the platform.

Most people cannot name the winners of the Super Bowl for the last twenty years. Neither can they name the World Series champions, nor the NBA, nor the World Cup. But I can still see the faces and name the names of my very first friends who got a divorce, as well as all the friends since then. There are at least twenty. And most of them are Christians. I can also see and name those sons and daughters of my friends who, having grown tired of the horrible family fights in their homes, chose to go elsewhere.

Try this exercise. Write down all the names of the people you love who have decided they no longer love each other. Make a list. Study it. Ask the logical questions that such a list should evoke.

- ★ Did my friends ever imagine they would end up divorced when they were standing at the altar?
- ★ What was their first fight like? How did it pave the way for a second?
- ★ How might things have been different if they followed the advice of Atticus Finch and simply said in their hearts, "It's not time to worry yet"—not time to be angry, or fuss, or fight?

Timing is everything.

I wish I'd had these thoughts tattooed on my heart that first night when I came home to Peter and he was so excited about the drawer.

It was a cold night out there in the garage—taking everything back out of the drawer again, recategorizing all the screws and washers and miscellaneous fasteners, grouping Phillips with Phillips and flatheads with flatheads, dumping the bits of trash, and hair, and leaves, and cheese, and…

Cheese? I looked a little closer. There in the bottom of the drawer, blending in perfectly with the wood, were shreds of moldy Kraft cheese from the garbage can...and a hundred tiny mouse droppings. And not only were there droppings, but a hole in the bottom corner of the drawer, just large enough for...

A mouse.

I have never understood why Peter so willingly took the rap for a measly rodent. Maybe he knew instinctively she was building a nest, doing what parents always do when winter is at hand—protecting her young from the cold. Maybe he didn't want to rat on her. Maybe he was afraid I'd give her a spanking, too.

Of course Peter forgave me when I finally figured it all out, and ran to his room, and got down on my knees right next to his little bed, and woke him up, and rambled on and on about what a schmuck I had been. After we talked for a long time, I kissed him and told him I loved him, and when I was almost to the door, I heard him say, "I love you, too, Daddy."

Kids are funny like that. I think that if every marriage were made up of two kindergartners, there'd be a lot less divorce. Sure, they'd fight over stuff like who gets the last bowl of Cap'n Crunch, or whether Batman could beat up Catwoman. And of course, because they're kids they'd be guilty of offsides fifty times a day. But just think how short their fights would be.

Kids know the value of time. They may not know the value of a tax return, or why Aunt Agnes shakes her finger whenever they stand on the furniture with muddy shoes, or why beds are meant for sleeping and not for jumping. But they can tell you the price of a sleepover with a friend, or licking the cake batter off the beaters, or those last golden days of a Christmas holiday, when leftovers are abundant and creatures pick scraps from the trash…and time scurries by on mouse legs.

Timing is everything.

And everything revolves around time.

Kids know these things.

Do you?

Do I?

There is a right time and a wrong time to have a fight—and now is almost always not the time.

LIGHT THE FUSE AND GET AWAY

God is patient. His timing is always perfect. If this were not so, I think He would have gotten fed up with my foolishness a long time ago, and knocked me into some adjacent galaxy.

I wish I were patient like God.

I also wish my timing weren't so cattywhompus. Some of the people with whom I have lost my temper wish this, too. Most of them were clients of mine at a residential treatment center. One of them had the habit of announcing to everyone that he could beat me up.

"You know I can take you," Chad enjoyed saying, especially on nights when we were packed into the center's small dining room and his comments were on display for the masses.

One evening Chad went too far. "The only reason you won't fight me is because you're scared," he said.

I felt my blood pressure surge. "Chad, I don't think it's in our best interest to continue this conversation."

"Really?" said Chad. He glanced at my two young sons, who were eating next to us at the table. "Well, I'm concerned about the best interest of your boys. I mean, you don't want them to grow up thinking their old man is a woman."

Wesley looked up from his spaghetti.

"This conversation is over," I replied.

Chad smirked. "I suppose you're right. Nobody should be forced to watch his old man back down from a fight."

I saw red. "Stand up, Chad," I said.

"Are we doing this now?" said Chad gleefully. With fists doubled, he stood up from the table and faced me.

The men's house director also stood up, with a look on his face that said, *Will? Are you sure you know what you're doing here?*

"Get the gloves, Sean," I told him.

"Oh, you want to do it with *gloves?"* said Chad. "That's fine with me. We can do it in the front yard, so everyone can watch me knock you into next week."

I stepped around the table, drawing up to within an inch of Chad's handsome face.

"How about if we box in the Boys' House living room—is that all right with you? It's a small space…not much room to run. Besides, it'd probably be best for you not to have too many people watching. Maybe just you and me; and we'll invite Sean to keep it on the safe side."

"Can I come, too, Daddy?" asked Wesley.

"Eat your spaghetti, son," I replied.

In the Boys' House, the living room was deafeningly quiet, except for the soft sounds of Chad and me tying on our gloves. Sean acted as the trainer for both corners, making sure our gloves were tight, filling us in on what he thought were rules for a fair fight, and doing his best to talk us out of it. Since we had no bell, Sean set his stopwatch and shouted, "Go!"

I do not remember much of the details after that—only the broad strokes of a fight that was over before it started. I charged straight across the room, leading with two left jabs and a right hook to Chad's face that sent him into the fireplace. I recall his looking puzzled, as if he hadn't counted on it happening this way.

I changed stances and hit him with a hard right lead to his nose, and this time the look I saw in his eyes was one of panic and hatred. It was then I knew our therapy sessions would never again be productive; but I couldn't bring myself to care at the moment. Again and again I hit Chad, until I was conscious of a thick forearm trying to separate the two of us, and Sean's faint voice.

"That's enough, Will," he said. "I think he's had enough."

On one of the couches that had formed our makeshift ring, Chad was slumped over with his head between his knees. For a moment I thought of saying something sarcastic to him, as a reminder that he ought to choose his battles more wisely next time. But suddenly I wasn't feeling so tough anymore; I felt like a thirty-year-old man picking on a boy.

True to my suspicions, Chad and I never connected well in counseling after that. Had I taken the time to know him, I might have figured out that to Chad public opinion was everything. Too bad my own interest in public opinion led me into sin. A month later, he was busted for drugs and had to leave the treatment center.

I am forty-six now, and I haven't heard from Chad since those days.

So many of our fights are the result of bad timing—haste, if you will. I suppose this is why Cindy and I began this whole athletic metaphor with the offsides rule. It was the first rule we developed, and it is usually the first rule we break in our own fights.

God is so long-suffering with us. He is the opposite of everything I exhibited in my fight with Chad. Looking back, I realize how easy it was for me to justify my actions. Even as I type the details of Chad's mockery, I feel my blood pressure rising.

Maybe you feel for me, too, thinking Chad got what he deserved. If so, then you must understand you are at odds with God's Word. James 1:19–20 says, "Everyone should be quick to listen, slow to speak and slow to become angry, for man's anger does not bring about the righteous life that God desires."

I wonder now if that's why Chad had no second thoughts in challenging me. Maybe he knew he would get pounded, and that knowledge gave him power.

Sometimes I wonder if I am just like Chad to God. I resist His love. I reject His counsel. I sass Him and mock His authority, acting as if I could lick Him in a fight.

The truth is if God ever punched me, I wouldn't be able to survive it. But instead, He's quick to listen, slow to speak, and slow to become angry.

God's timing is perfect. He is never offsides—not with me, not with you, not with Chad or the Israelites. Someday His anger will be kindled against an unbelieving world, but not just yet. You and I still have time to lengthen our fuses, time to bring our anger to a snail's pace, and time to quit violating the Offsides rule.

If timing is everything in a family fight, then you must become aware of those times when your fuse is shortest. My own are as follows:

★ Anytime after 10 p.m.
★ Anytime I've been embarrassed or disrespected (especially in public).
★ Anytime someone messes up the "order" I've worked hard to achieve.

I could easily make excuses for getting angry in these "short fuse times." But just as anger wounds the loved one, excuses only pour salt in those wounds. My family does not need to hear my excuses; my family needs me to quit jumping offsides and penalizing our team.

So here is what we do in my family: When the clock strikes ten, I am not permitted to notice the dishes in the sink, or the clothes that still need folding, or the fact that my workbench drawer is out of order again.

I am only permitted to enjoy the end of the day—read a book, play X-Box with my boys, rub Cindy's feet, pray with the family, and slowly drift off into the pillow.

Habanero

Delay of Game

The ear is a woman's most sensitive erogenous zone; do not listen to a woman unless you want her to be seriously attracted to you.

The other day I was in a restaurant that offered a ridiculous variety of hot sauces. Sixty-three bottles lined the counter. I know this because I counted them all, searching the labels for a clue as to which was the hottest. I hoped the names would provide an answer, but they all seemed equally sinister:

"Hotter than Hades"

"Fire in the Hole"

"Mike's Insanity"

"Wanna try one?" asked the kid behind the counter, his apron splotched with a selection of sauces.

"No, thanks. I'm just looking," I replied.

I continued down the line, rotating bottles and scanning their labels. But now I was aware of the kid's eyes following me.

"You won't find it there," he said at last.

"'It'?"

"Yeah, 'it'—the hottest sauce in the house. We keep it in the refrigerator."

The kid disappeared behind a stainless steel door, then reemerged holding an unremarkable little bottle. The label had no ominous flames, no gasping caricature of the last poor schlepper who dared to taste it.

Nevertheless, something about the way the kid held the bottle—two fingers around its slender neck, and slightly away from his body—told me the stuff was for real.

"Why don't you keep it on the counter with the rest of the bottles?" I asked.

"I think it has something to do with insurance or lawsuits. We've had this same bottle in the fridge since we opened three years ago. Only two people have tried it. You want to be the third?"

"Not today."

"We'll put your name on a plaque," he offered, pointing to a greasy, nondescript piece of plywood that immortalized the names of the two men who had succumbed to the urging of fellow cowards.

Our eyes met, and for a moment I thought I saw the look of someone who has the habit of slowing down to gawk at car wrecks—and hasn't seen a good one in a while.

I must admit that at that moment pride threw a lure into the pool of my wretched soul and almost reeled me in. But two things caused me to resist the temptation: the distant memory of a similar experience years ago in Memphis, and the uncontrollable urge to teach this boy a lesson.

"Have you ever lost a farkle?" I asked.

"You mean, like Paper-Rock-Scissors?"

"That's it."

"I win some, I lose some."

"Yeah. Me, too. But once I was with some pals in Memphis, and I lost one so bad I'll never forget it."

The kid set the bottle down and leaned forward on the counter, eager to hear about my misfortune.

"So we're all gathered around this table at a barbecue joint on Beale Street. Suddenly I get this notion that we need to farkle, and whoever loses the farkle has to do a dance around the restaurant, real slow-like, and with a mambo touch to it. So everybody agrees."

"And you lost?" asked the kid excitedly.

"Well, no…not directly."

"I thought you said you lost."

"Actually, one of my pals lost."

"So, did he do the farkle?"

"Not at first. You see, he had this one condition. He made me promise that if he did the dance, I had to do whatever he asked when he finished…or else I'm a weasel for the rest of my life."

The kid leaned closer to me and smirked. "Your friend must be a real jerk," he said.

"Not really. I mean, you can't take every little word a person says seriously. Anyway, not wanting to be a weasel, I agreed to his terms, and off he went. It's an excellent dance as far as obnoxious public behavior goes, and to be honest, I was proud as heck of him. He took his sweet time, you know, dipping in between tables, weaving to avoid waiters, even pausing to give private performances for a couple on their first date and a family with small children. When he finally returned to our table, he'd been gone so long that I completely forgot about my end of the bargain. That's when I realized I'd made a very big mistake."

"What happened?"

"Hold your horses," I said. "I'm getting to it."

All the while I had my eye on that little bottle, and an evil plot was hatching in my brain.

"Where was I?"

"The very big mistake."

"Right. Thanks. Anyway, when my buddy got back to our table, he had this wicked grin on his face, like the most diabolical idea had just come over him. I noticed all the other guys were grinning, too. Without hesitating, my buddy grabbed his backpack and whipped out the biggest, fattest, nastiest habanero pepper I'd ever seen in my life. And he pointed to the pepper and said, 'Would you like some fries with that, Mr. Weasel?'"

"Ha ha ha ha ha," laughs the kid, his skinny, pipe cleaner legs pumping out an evil jig. "That's the funniest trick I've ever heard."

"Oh, I thought so, too."

"Did you know the habanero is the fourth hottest pepper in the world?"

"You don't say."

"Yeah, it'll burn the taste right out of your mouth."

"You can say that again," I replied, adding a shudder for effect. I knew the path down which I was leading the kid, and frankly, the longer I was in his presence, the better I felt about my decision. "Fourth hottest or not, I can tell you from experience it's a good thing you keep that bottle separate from the others."

The kid's eyes narrowed with skepticism.

"Don't tell me you ate that pepper."

"All right, I won't tell you."

"You *ate* a habanero?"

"The whole thing."

"No way."

"Way."

"What'd it feel like?"

"Like the devil riding a lawn mower down my esophagus."

"You are *the man!*"

"Well, I don't know about that," I said, "but I will tell you that once a fellow does something really crazy, like eating a whole habanero, nothing ever seems quite as scary again."

"Wow," whispered the kid reverently, as if I were a god or something. "Hey, are you going to order a sandwich?"

I half expected that he'd give it to me free of charge, but I wasn't really hungry. "Nah, I was just stopping in to use your restroom. But…"

And here is where my evil plot cracked out of its shell and stood on the counter like a giant gargoyle. Ignoring it was not an option.

"Since we're on the topic," I said, "why don't you and I farkle to see who takes a taste of your sauce?"

The kid glanced in horror at the bottle on the counter, then smiled weakly. "You're kidding, right?"

"Actually, I'm not."

His smile disappeared. "Okay, I'm game, I guess. I'm just not sure what my manager would say about it."

"We'll be careful," I assured him. "Besides…just think, one of us is going to get his name on the plaque. Do you have any crackers?"

The kid produced a packet of Saltines, removed one, and slathered it with the greenish-black nuclear waste. Then we both stuck out our fists and steeled ourselves for the verdict.

"We'll throw on three," I said.

The kid had closed his eyes.

"One, two, *three*."

Now, I will never know this for sure, because the lighting in that place had grown dimmer during our conversation. But when the kid opened his eyes and saw that his scissors had lost to my rock, I am almost positive he turned the color of oatmeal.

"I don't want to be a weasel," he said, reaching for the cracker with his trembling hand.

"Nobody does," I consoled.

Not one for car wrecks, I left that establishment before the kid had swallowed the second half of the cracker. The last image I have is of his face turning crimson and his pell-mell rush for the restroom. I knew exactly what he was going through—and what was going through him, too.

Poor kid, I thought. *He'll be feeling that habanero twice. Once on the way in, and once on the way—*

Well, we'll leave it at that. Let's just say that for learning one of life's most valuable lessons, there is no teacher quite like the habanero.

Now...picture yourself in a huddle.

Of course, if you are a woman reading this book, I am asking you to work with me here. I know it is not normal for women to be in football huddles, surrounded by stinking, sweating, cussing beasts. It might even be hard for you to imagine it.

In all honesty, that is the same way I feel when I go to buy my wife a nightgown at one of your lingerie stores—without all the sweat and swear words, of course.

One of the smartly dressed women always asks me the same question: "Can I help you with something?"

I don't know why she has to phrase it that way. If I answer with, "No...I'm just looking," then I immediately become the front-runner in the perv pool that she and her friends have going on behind the counter.

Almost from birth we men have figured out that "looking" is acceptable at Sears or Home Depot, but not in this store. We've decided that the best way to handle ourselves in the smartly dressed woman's store is not to look at all, but rather to shuffle along with our heads down, hoping something will jump off the rack and magically race to the counter, where we can act like we are just stopping in to ask for directions to the chainsaw store, or the kiosk where they sell elk urine to hunters.

This way, we can glance down at the counter and "suddenly" notice the frilly, lacy, awesomely thin little item that has materialized there and say to the smartly dressed woman with as much casualness as we can muster, "Hey, while you're at it, why not wrap up one of these ol' rags, here, and I'll take it home for the missus."

But it doesn't always work out this way.

If, for instance, I have slipped into a mild coma, and have suddenly forgotten what kind of store I am in when the smartly dressed woman asks her question, then I will answer, "Yes, ma'am. I'm looking for something for my wife." And then before I know it, I am in a conversation with a complete stranger, talking about things that complete strangers should not be talking about.

"If you don't mind my asking, how big is your wife?"

"Oh...about this big," I say, holding up my hand to where I think the top of Cindy's head should be, if she were barefoot and wearing the type of thing Smart Dresser and I are sinfully discussing.

"Do you know her size?"

"She's more on the smallish size."

Smartie sighs. "Have you bought her teddies before?"

At this point I feel my face rushing toward redness, like a

person who thought he was biting into a Twinkie and then finds out it's a habanero.

"Excuse me?" I say, not wanting to admit I've heard of teddies before, much less have a history of purchasing them. I don't even like the sound of the word *teddy*—it sounds like it was invented by a couple of junior high boys under a bridge.

Smartie sighs again. "If I hold it up to me *like this,* would it help?"

She brings the frilly, lacy, awesomely thin little item to rest against her extremely-attractive-but-not-my-wife's bosom. I don't need to see her hold it up *like this,* or *like that,* or any other way. What I need for her to do, if she really wants to make a sale, is to crumple the thing up and throw it over in the corner against the wall, which is how I am familiar with such an item anyway.

Smartie clears her throat, as if to get my attention again.

"Sir?"

"Hmm?"

"Have you made your decision?"

"Yes, ma'am. I have decided to go see Dave at Sears."

"Dave?" says Smartie.

"Dave is a big fat salesman who works in Lawn and Garden, and who stinks and sweats and cusses for no good reason, and makes me feel comfortable whenever I shop in his department."

"What could you possibly buy for your wife from Dave?"

"The Martha Stewart weed eater."

Smartie turns her nose up. "Your wife is one lucky woman."

"You better believe it."

I begin my slow grope toward the store entrance—except I do not want to touch a single pair of socks, because that would activate the Perv Alert, and not even Mike Ditka could fight his way through a roadblock of smartly dressed women.

What I'm attempting to say here is that habaneros, huddles, and hosiery shops have more in common than I used to think. They can each be intimidating if you haven't had much experience with them.

Here is some advice to make the football huddle more comfortable for everyone:

1. Listen.
2. Don't say a word.
3. And then listen some more.

Contrary to belief, huddles are not town hall meetings, where everyone from linebackers to lingerie salesmen are free to express their opinion. In the huddle, only one person is allowed to speak, and that is the quarterback.

"Cunningham, line up in the slot and run a deep post. Simpson, the play-action is coming to you. Sell the fake like crazy this time, and dive off tackle. Get to the flat fast. You're my go-to if I get in a pickle. Tipps, split out left, and run a streak. And for the love of everything that is decent, Dunwoodie, do not forget to pick up the blitz."

All of this has to happen flawlessly at least several dozens times during a football game, in spite of the fans yelling, the clock ticking, and whole seasons on the line. You can see why listening in the huddle is so important, and also why the air rushes out of the crowd whenever a referee blows his whistle and says the dreaded words: "Delay of game!"

More than any other penalty in the book, Delay of Game is painfully counterproductive.

Remember—input always determines output. Just as *listening in a huddle* leads to success on the field, and the *input of a habanero* leads to a swift and certain output, healthy family fights demand that one person at a time has the floor.

This is only possible when, like a football team, each family member has the common goal of getting to the end zone.

Kids grow brains when they turn twelve years old. When this miracle happened to our sons, I had to make some adjustments in the huddle. Overnight, it seemed, Wes and Peter became serious contenders for the quarterback position. And I was threatened.

At first I simply talked louder and in run-on sentences; and for a while it worked. But as our boys got older and wanted to find out what their new brains could do, our team morale grew unpleasant.

One day Cindy gave me some simple advice. "Maybe they have some good things to say, honey. Maybe you ought to show them you are listening by rephrasing the things they tell you."

"You mean use the same advice I give in my counseling office?"

"Yeah, that might work."

Cindy is pretty sharp, so I thought I would give it a try.

It's funny how counselors are always the last ones to follow their own wisdom. Things instantly got better, and over the years I have stuck to my wife's advice with only the occasional relapse into idiocy. Now when Wes wants to negotiate a curfew, I don't feel as if I immediately have to assume the quarterback role. Usually when I listen closely and rephrase his case to him, I find that both of us soften, become more open to each other's viewpoints, and arrive at a winning compromise.

"Dad, I'm thinking of going to a movie tonight with Baker."

"I thought you had homework to do."

"I do, but Baker is leaving town tonight and I probably won't see him for a while."

"It sounds like that relationship is pretty important to you."

"Yeah, it is. But, I figure I can block out some time on Sunday afternoon to get my homework done."

"Great. What movie are you going to see?"

"The Texas Chainsaw Massacre."

"Super. Have a nice time."

"Dad?"

"Yeah, son?"

"I'm just kidding about the chainsaw thing."

"I know."

Huddles are so much more fun when we listen to one another. But does this mean a family must be run by committee, with a huddle that is cluttered by the voices of multiple quarterbacks? One could look at it that way.

We have four quarterbacks in the Cunningham family, all with keen ability to contribute ideas and make decisions. But we always follow the rule of "one at a time." And, of course, I am still the head coach. Sometimes after listening to my sons and finding their thoughts shot full of holes, I still have to impose my will over theirs.

The nice thing is that they receive my coach's prerogative more readily because I have received their attempts at quarterback more frequently.

This is active listening, and the more we practice it, the less likely we are to violate Delay of Game. Later in the book we'll look at Goal Tending and discuss what to do when someone we love has a really, really bad idea, like wanting to get a tattoo the size of Rhode Island between his shoulder blades.

But for now, we'll just work on the easier stuff.

CHUP LIKE A PUPPLE BUD

I used to be "cute as a bug," according to our next-door neighbor.

Now that I'm grown up and have hair growing from my ears, I think that the "cute as a bug" analogy is a very strange one. I've seen some bugs in my lifetime, and none of them were cute. Poisonous, maybe, or annoying, or disgusting—but never cute.

Why do we do this to the English language—assign adjectives to nouns that are neither fitting nor necessary? Have we forgotten that words mean things, and that they carry within them the seeds of war and diplomacy?

Bugs are not cute. Neither are buttons, or pie, or the girl who is "as cute as can be." If she's as cute as she can be, then she has reached the glass ceiling of cuteness, and all the makeup in the world, piled up and plastered on her face, cannot make her any cuter. She is Quasimodo in a camisole, feeling slightly better about herself because we have told her she is "as cute as can be."

Words mean things, and listening to them can mean the difference between a good fight and a bad fight. Delay of Game is what happens when we refuse to listen. The penalty is simple: prolonged pain.

The kind of listening I am talking about is different from the kind necessary to avoid being offsides. A wide receiver can spring from the line of scrimmage at the right time and still run the wrong pattern. Why? Because he did not understand the quarterback's instructions in the huddle.

Similarly, it is a beautiful thing to be "slow to speak, and slow to become angry"—but one can hold his tongue all day long and never really understand the meaning of the words coming from his neighbor's mouth.

Listening requires understanding.

Sometimes the only way one can understand a message he receives is to take it into his *own* mouth, roll it around with his tongue until the flavor of individual words becomes distinguishable, and then finally spit it back out so that the person who sent the message can know whether he has been understood. This is "active listening," and it is the only way to avoid Delay of Game.

"It hurts me when you don't use the cereal bowl I set out for you the night before."

"Cindy, I'm trying to understand you, but it's hard in this case. Why would something that seems so small bother you so greatly?"

"Because when you overlook the bowl that's already on the counter, and just go grab another one from the cupboard, it makes me think you don't notice my service or…my love for you."

"So…this is deeper than I thought."

"Yes."

"It's a 'love thing.'"

"Yes."

"Wow." (Long pause.) "How?"

"Well…in my family, service was the greatest way we showed love."

"You mean, like all those grapefruits your dad has been cutting up every night for, like, fifty years? That's a lot of grapefruits. Have you ever thought about how many—"

"Yes, Will, I've thought about it; I've *lived* it. My dad cut up four grapefruits every night, and sprinkled sugar on them so they'd be ready the following morning for each family member. And he did it because he loved us."

"What happened when grapefruit season was over?"

"He switched to cantaloupes. I think you're missing the point, Will."

"No, I've got it. What you're trying to say with the cereal bowl is that you love me."

"Yes."

"And you don't want me to reject your love."

"Yes!"

"I am a really smart man."

(Conspicuously long pause.)

"Well, that's why I married you."

★ ★ ★

Everybody wants to be understood, but not everybody wants to understand. This is a teenager's number one complaint about his parents.

When Peter was a little boy and I was quietly dying in my counseling practice, he had a lisp that was cute.

Please note that I did *not* say, "Peter was cute as a lisp." Lisps are often sources of embarrassment for the lisper, impediments that crowd the waiting rooms of speech pathologists, or hindrances that bar one's road to Broadway.

In general, there is nothing cute about lisps.

Still, it is my prerogative to lift a singular lisp out of the boatload of lisping done on Planet Earth and enshrine it on the throne of cuteness, just as it is your prerogative to bend down and root around in the grass until you find a particular bug you believe is a real cutie. But shame on you and me if we try to convince each other that *all* bugs and *all* lisps are equally cute.

Shame on me, too, for leading you off on this bunny trail. There is nothing cute about a writer who forces his reader to explore his world of free association. It's just that this word thing is so important to me.

And apparently it was important to my son, Peter, one day when he was five, and we were sitting in a pool together.

"Daddy?"

"Hm?"

"Jimmy says I talk funny."

"That's mean and terrible."

"What should I do?"

"I think you should tell Jimmy that he's fat, and someday all his blubber is going to suffocate his heart."

"Should I really tell him that?"

"No, not really."

"Daddy?"

"Hm?"

"Do you think I talk funny?"

"I don't know, son—say something."

"What should I say?"

"Say *bird.*"

"Bud."

"Sounds good to me. Maybe Jimmy just speaks a different language than you—like French, or Japanese, or the stuff that Daddy says when he drops a bird feeder on his toe. Do you understand what Daddy is trying to say, here?"

"Mm-hm."

"Good. Would you like to learn Jimmy's language, so the two of you can communicate better?"

"Okay."

"All righty, then. Let's start with the word *bird,* which is the way people pronounce it in Jimmish. You, of course, pronounce it 'bud,' which is perfectly cool and functional in the land of Peter. Am I making sense?"

"Yes."

"Go ahead and say *bird.*"

"Bud."

"Fantastic. Now let's think of some other words that have the same sounds as *bird.* Let me see, now. I wonder, wonder, wonder. Okay, I've got it. How about 'chirp' and 'purple'? Can you say *chirp?*"

"Chup."

"Excellent. Now try *purple.*"

"Pupple."

"Peter Cunningham, you are the King of Linguistics."

"I've never *hud* of him."

"I'll bet you haven't. The fact of the matter is, a lot of people have never *hud* of him. But you're him—King Ling. And you are halfway down the path to bilingualism."

"What's bi—?"

"It doesn't matter; let's keep learning. Okay—this time I want you to string all three words together, and keep saying them until they come out exactly like this: Chiiiirp…like a puu-uurple….biiiird."

"Chup like a pupple bud."

"Chirp."

"Chup."

"Errrrrrrrrrr."

"Uhhhhhhhhh."

"Astounding. Now off you go. Chirp like a purple bird. Keep chirping."

We were in our neighbor's pool at the time, and to be perfectly candid my mind was anywhere *but* on the topic of my son's cute lisp. Cindy and I had lived with it ever since Peter began to talk and just assumed he'd outgrow it someday.

What I was thinking about that day, actually *worrying* about as I watched Peter chupping happily around the pool, was whether God really cared about my plight as a melancholy marriage counselor. I had been talking to Him for months, trying to organize my complaints in just such a way that He would take action and free me from the bonds of counsel.

It's not that I wasn't skilled at counseling, or that I didn't think it would enable me to pay the bills; it's just that after twelve years of sitting in an office with unhappy couples, a great deal of their unhappiness had rubbed off on me—like mud from a cranky old man's shoe.

"Chup like a pupple bud!" sang Peter, as he floated past me on a raft.

I wondered if God had heard me chupping all these long months. Did He really listen to people's prayers—I mean, individual people and individual prayers? Or did He only field ones uttered by special people, clerical types who knew where to insert the "thee's" and "thou's" and "beseecheth's"? Would He really take notice of a chuckleheaded chupper like myself?

"Chup like a pupple bud!"

"Keep chupping, son," I called.

I did not grow up with a lot of active listening; I don't think anybody my age did. Parents of my generation were more into *doing* than *saying*, so words and their meaning didn't seem as important to them.

Maybe it stemmed from the Great Depression or the World Wars, those times when folks were too busy fighting for food and freedom to give much thought to communication. Whatever the case, nobody of alleged wisdom was telling my generation anything of importance—like how we ought to have quiet times, or kiss dating good-bye, or limit our intake of Alice Cooper. The extent of worship music at our youth groups was "One Tin Soldier" and "House of the Rising Sun." Do you understand the poverty I'm describing here?

Deep in my heart I am thankful to my elders for stemming the tide of fascism and pulling this country up by its bootstraps. But besides safety and nourishment, we were not given much verbal instruction on how to climb the ladder to a happy marriage or a holy friendship with God.

Words are so important.

He who cherishes the understanding of words gets filthy rich with wisdom.

"Chirp like a purple bird!" blurted Peter suddenly.

He was so excited that he fell off the raft. When he resurfaced, he was chirping the phrase over and over—perfectly. "I did it, Daddy!"

"Yes you did, my little man," I replied.

"Jimmy can't say I talk funny anymore."

"No, he can't. The King of Ling has mastered a whole new language."

That night the family celebrated with a trip to Baskin-Robbins. Later on when I was tucking Peter into bed, he told me that the "fust" thing he was going to do in the morning was give Jimmy a call and tell him about his accomplishment.

Clearly, we still had work to do.

Nevertheless, Cindy and I went to bed rejoicing over Peter's new ability. We also took the time to kneel and ask God one more time to hear my prayers about counseling, and I am sorry to admit that it was probably Cindy's faith that got His attention.

The next morning I received a call from a friend in Missouri, wondering whether I would be interested in a position as a camp director.

"I'll need to think about it," I said. "All right, when do I start?"

Nine years later, I'm still running around in shorts and tennis shoes, playing with kids, and wondering why I ever doubted that God listens.

God always listens.

He does not always answer in the way I want, or on my time schedule, but He always listens and He always understands.

Listening to one another in a family fight is as vital to a home as it was to brave Daniel in the lion's den, or barren Elizabeth waiting for a son, or bitter Saul with his scaly eyes.

God heard Daniel and shut the lions' mouths. He lingered on Elizabeth's requests for motherhood and gave her John the Baptist. He bent low to Saul's ear and whispered, "I have heard your zeal for the Law—now show Me what a man of your caliber can do when he is zealous for My love."

And the scales fell off. The scales always fall off when we listen to one another.

For four long centuries God listened to the Israelites in

Egyptian captivity, holding His ear to their cries like a tuning fork until they struck the repentant chord He was waiting for; then He set them free. I used to wonder what the Israelites thought of God during those four hundred years. Maybe they thought He was deaf, or on vacation, or just plain mean. But I don't think any of those things anymore. Now I think the problem with listening was Israel's, not God's.

God also listened to Abraham; and Abraham listened back. Maybe this is why he was called the Father of Israel. Maybe God had been waiting and watching for someone who was interested in a two-way conversation, and along came Abraham.

Maybe that's why God blessed Abraham with Isaac—so that he would teach his boy how to listen. And then Isaac would do the same with Jacob, and Jacob with his twelve sons, and on and on, all the way up to now.

It's possible.

But I don't know much.

I'm just a bird—a happy, chirping, purple bird who is glad to know that God listens to my "chups."

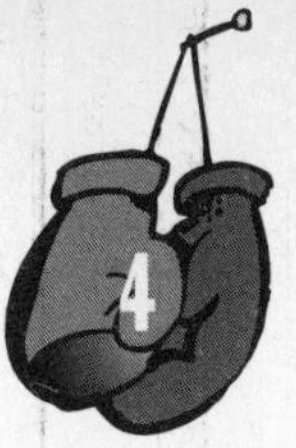

Shufflin' Off to Buffalo

BACKFIELD IN MOTION

Backfield in Motion is what happens when a player moving parallel to the line veers toward the line before the ball is snapped. It also happens every time I remind my wife of the time she wrecked our car in Colorado. This is usually when Cindy reminds me that the only thing I know how to cook is Pop-Tarts—and you can see where this is leading.

I would very much like for you to know me more by the end of this chapter.

Not because I am special, or an exhibitionist, but because I believe certain stories are common to us all. Like the illogical one about going to school in our underwear, or the terrifying one about monsters under our beds, or worst of all, the one about our homes becoming ghost towns someday when our children drive off to college in the cars we bought for them, saying, "See ya later, old man. I'll be back once a year at Christmas. So long—send money!"

Common stories are sometimes the most deeply buried ones. They do not need a storyteller; they need a grave robber. Someone who is willing to put a boot to a spade, and hoist whatever he finds down there into the light.

I am writing this evening in the mood of such a man. It hangs about my shoulders like a mildewed jacket: heavy, wet, perfect for the job ahead. I am mad as heck at my oldest son right now.

Scratch that. My oldest son has hurt me, and now I want to hurt him back.

This is a dangerous thing to say, seeing as I am standing here with this spade in my hand. But someone has to do the digging. Lord knows I've always appreciated it when a comrade has the courage to exhume something that was stinking in his life. Such courage has often inspired me to do some digging of my own. So, here I dig.

What stinks most is that Wes and I used to be buddies. We built tree houses together, mowed mazes into the shoulder-high grass next door, rode bikes, went to the zoo, played with Legos.

These thoughts are thick as clay. It hurts my mind to will them out of the hole where they live. But I do not want dead things living under my house.

I have dug this far before and stopped. Here are signs of my previous digging—a memory of a fishing trip sliced in half by the blunt edge of my impatience.

"Wesley! If I've told you once, I've told you forty-seven times: Be careful with other peoples' things! Now you've gone and broken the tip off my best rod. What were you thinking?"

I do not know why parents ask this question. It's like it has been included in the *Official Guide to Language for Parents* and we all feel obliged to use it. I wonder what it would sound like if a kid ever answered it with the kind of honor it deserves.

"Well actually, Dad, what I was really thinking was that I'd rather be having a root canal right now than fishing with you. I'd rather walk on broken glass. I'd rather my entire body be made out of chalkboard, and have all the seniors at school scratch their fingernails down me. I'd rather climb to the top of a ladder, staple my eyelids to the ceiling, and then have someone pull the ladder out from under me. *That's* what I was thinking. That's pretty much it in a nutshell."

I'm sorry, my friend. The book was sailing along so nicely, and now I have brought it to a numbing pace, like Eeyore crashing Pooh's birthday party. But I beg you not to walk away from this hole where I am digging and ranting. I am hopeful something down here might benefit you.

There! Over there in the shadows! I see a half-eaten plate of scrambled eggs, a reminder of an evening when I made Wesley sit in his chair until midnight over a stupid, stupid rule that was drummed into my head as a child. EAT EVERYTHING ON YOUR PLATE—OR SOMEHOW THE STARVING CHILDREN IN AFRICA WILL STARVE FASTER.

If I had a stamp for every time I sat in the dark, staring at spinach marinated in tears, I could have boxed it up and saved Botswana. The worst part is that Wes hates eggs to this day. Why is it we repeat our parents' mistakes with our oldest children? Why do we do the very things to them that we couldn't stand? Why am I here digging it all up again?

I know why.

I suspect if I dig long enough, I will come to an even older layer of memories, compressed beneath this one that always halts my digging. If I could stand back from this task, get a cross-section of it all from a better vantage point, I imagine it might look to me like the limestone cliffs on Highway 65 between Branson and Springfield.

Layer of lime.
Layer of mud.
Layer of lime.
Layer of mud.

I live with the hope that somewhere beneath me, fossilized into the layers yet to come, are the perfectly kept remains of my ancient friendship with my oldest son—whole days of laughter, hugs untainted by apology, winks, nods, nudges, smiles, all of them asleep like a fallen dinosaur.

Here is something. My shovel hits it with a solid *thud,* not with the squishy sound of dead things. I begin to dig like a badger, fingers clawing, nails whittling down to nubs, dirt flying, until at last I come to what I am looking for—a memory so golden it could wipe out the poverty of my attitude toward Wes. Water pours now into the hole, where I am squatting like a miner with his find.

I pick it up and cradle it in my hands.

Dearest of memories, I have been looking for you. But to think I would discover you here, rinsed clean by time and subterranean springs…it is almost intoxicating.

I do not know why this memory means so much to me, or why I dig to retrieve it whenever life gets painful with Wes. Maybe it's because it reflects a thing that happened to me once with my own father.

I was three, with no business being in the neighbor's pool. He was thirty-eight, a golden light shaft piercing down through other shafts of lesser gold, until he reached me where I lay drowning on the drain—watching and waiting for him. I knew he would come. It was not time to die, yet.

Most of human bonding has its roots in water.

★ ★ ★

The memory my spade has just struck begins on a river—one of the six trips we took down the Buffalo. Or was it one of the three on the North Fork? Water has such a way of washing things, including the recollection of them. It doesn't matter. Take any of these adventures, and you would have found me teaching my boy something new—how to paddle a canoe, how to shoot a BB gun, how to tell the difference between a coral and a king snake.

Red 'n' black, friend-o'-jack.

Red 'n' yella, kill a fella.

There were nights the stars were so thick, they looked like a down comforter spread over the hills by one of those moms who perpetually smells like sugar cookies.

"That's Cassiopeia over there, son."

"It looks like a *w*."

"Of course it does. I had a talk with Stan about it."

"Who's Stan, Daddy?"

"Stan the star guy. You know Stan. You've probably just forgotten him. Anyway, I told him, 'Look here, Stan, old pal, I sure would appreciate it if you threw together a few stars for me to remember my boy by.' So Stan says that wouldn't be too much trouble, and—BINGO! The next night there she is, five stars in a shining *w*, made especially for you, Wesley."

"Is that true, Daddy?"

"If it's not, it should be."

I crack myself up writing these last six words, because I heard them so many times from my own dad, at the close of his nightly forgeries. Bedtime stories were my introduction to a foundational truth about the world, that much of what we know is built on the footings of white lies—harmless, sugared narratives, occasionally sliced into by a child's suspicion, then iced over again and again. Twain called them "stretchers," and I will argue with anyone who says they do any serious harm to little boys and girls. If anything, they restore the wonder we adults have scrubbed God's world clean of.

The ability to entertain on a shoestring runs deep in my family. One of my ancestors was the original storyteller in caveman days.

Now, it is true that many words lead to much sin. But the gift of words properly wielded is from God, and it must have some purpose for the Cunningham family; because anywhere you go in the world you will eventually find one of us entertaining someone around a fire. My own dad was the king of one-liners.

1. "If I've told you once, I've told you forty-seven times" came straight from Dad, as did countless other sayings, some designed for discipline, most for diversion.

2. "You look like Maggie-off-the-pickle-boat" was invented to tell me that my hair looked like two cats had fought in it all night long, and would need to be de-furred and reattached to my head before we left for church. To this day I still believe there is such a thing as a pickle boat.

3. "Is that about the most fun you've ever had with your clothes on?" was a smidge of adult humor that found its way into my ears somehow. The only detrimental effect it had on me was that I tried it one night at the dinner table of my best friend's family, and they all looked at me like I was Hugh Hefner.

The following is my favorite.

4. "I'll tell you when I get to know you better" was Dad's standard answer to many ordinary questions.

For me as a child, this was an incentive to hurry up and get older so I could sit at my father's right hand, have conferred upon me all the knowledge of the neighborhood, and become immortal.

But when I became a father, I discovered the phrase had multiple interpretations and could be used for anything from "I am not in a mood to answer that question right now" to "I have no idea what you are talking about" to "Leave me alone."

This discovery had two effects on me. First, it reduced the number of mysteries swirling about my father by one; and second, it almost cost me my relationship with Cindy. Upon asking me a question once, and receiving Dad's standard answer, Cindy replied, "You won't *get* to know me better until you tell me what I want to know."

★ ★ ★

I think that while my ancestors were flicking boogers in the fire and making pterodactyls out of tissue paper, Cindy's ancestors were out taking over the world.

From then on, I always told Cindy what she wanted to know when she wanted to know it.

Anyway, on the morning of my dearest memory, I was entertaining Wesley as usual. The Buffalo River was dangerously high that spring, much too high for a three-year-old to be on it.

"I'll keep his life jacket on twenty-four hours a day," I promised Cindy as we waited to put in at Ponca Beach. She had that look in her eyes, the one that says, "I am married to a pirate, and he is about to steal my most prized possession."

"Are you sure he'll wear the jacket?" Cindy pressed.

"He'll wear the jacket."

"Are you telling me the truth?"

"If I'm not, I should be."

"Will!"

"Okay, okay. He will sleep with it on, eat with it on, go potty with it on. Wesley will become one with this jacket," I assured her.

Eventually she seemed convinced. We kissed, and hugged, and promised not to come home dead, and then we were off like Lewis and Clark and around the first bend before Mom could change her mind. Five minutes later, Wesley had the jacket off and was jumping out of the canoe in his underwear.

Much words. Much sin. Big, dumb, stupid, sinful pirate.

There were twelve of us dads with our sons on this trip, all seasoned vets of the Buffalo, all accomplished river rats. The air was pregnant with the smell of campfires and cinnamon apples, the rapids more treacherous than I had remembered. With a three-year-old in the bow, I had to generate both the power and the trajectory from my place in the stern. In such situations, only the J-stroke and a timely use of the rudder will do the trick. I had mastered both as a teenager and was feeling pretty good about myself.

I even stood up and taunted one of the rapids we vanquished, celebrating like a running back that has just crossed the goal line.

"Booo-yaw! You ain't so bad, Mr. Rapid! What? You want some of *me*? Are we doing this now? Say something!"

It was not mature dad behavior, but Wesley got a kick out of it. Suddenly, while I was still yelling at the water, our canoe scraped the most insignificant twig in the widest part of the river, and over we went.

I bobbed up, wet and sputtering, surrounded by coolers, lanterns, duffel bags, and two very soggy sleeping bags. Ahead of me I saw the keel of the canoe, knifing toward the next bend—and the next set of rapids. But no sign of Wesley.

The pirate panicked.

"He's under the canoe!" Joe White shouted. Joe is my

friend, and a very good boss, and the guy who taught me how to do the J-stroke when I was a teenager. He is much humbler than I, and would probably never have been patting himself on the back over some stupid rapids when he should have been watching the water ahead of him.

"Your boy is under the canoe!" he repeated.

Oh, God. Please… I thought, as I lunged forward with the current and swam with all my strength.

I think it is odd that we add "please" to our requests of God in situations like this. I am all for manners, but I do not think there is a special prayer etiquette—particularly for emergencies. Even odder is the possibility I was tacking "please" on to my cry for God to save Wesley because I did not expect His help without some measure of begging or a ceremonial gesture, like a curtsy or a kiss on His ring. All of this brings up a very good question.

Must a person plead with God to get His help? King David never pleaded. I believe he was a great king, and a man after God's heart and all, but let's face it: He was also pretty sick and selfish. He had sex with his good friend's wife, then had that good friend killed to cover up what he had done. If someone ought to be begging for God's help, it was David. But he never did. Psalm 51 shows him saying simply, "I am sick, God. I have always been sick. I am sorry for being sick. Restore me."

I believe God loves to help people who admit they are sickos—even if they don't say the magic word.

I also believe God is a multitasker. But six billion people, all making requests at once? That could be a bit much. How could God help them all? Wouldn't He have to do triage, and decide who needed His help the most? That could waste time, and people could die while God was helping someone else.

What if a really noble person, who had not sinned in years, was choking on a piece of lamb in Westminster, England, while at the same time this other fellow, say, maybe a fellow who had just told a lie about a life jacket, was flopping around like a whiskerfish in a whirlpool—would God choose Westminster guy over Whiskerfish?

I thought about these things as I struggled to reach Wesley in the Buffalo.

My friend Milton probably has some opinions on this topic, too. We were seminary students together back in the eighties. Once I asked another student, Gary, why a dismal cloud followed Milt everywhere he went. Gary looked at me as if I had just asked him the name of the first book in the Bible.

"You haven't heard?" he said.

"No, I haven't."

We were in the library, so Gary lowered his voice. But I also think he lowered it out of reverence for Milt.

"His oldest boy drowned on a canoe trip."

"That's awful."

"It's worse than awful. Milt was in the canoe with his son when it broadsided a root wad the size of an RV, and started taking on water."

I could've stopped Gary right there and finished the story for him, because I have been in that predicament before and I know how dangerous it is for a canoeist. But I let him go on.

"Milt grabbed the nearest root in the giant wad, but his boy got scared and leaned away from it, and…"

"The canoe went over," I whispered.

"Yeah, the canoe went over, and the kid was sucked beneath it, sucked to the bottom of the river."

We were both silent for a moment, glancing around to make sure Milt wasn't in a nearby study cubicle. Gary's eyes started to tear up. It was the first time I'd seen a guy cry since my freshman year in college, when Elliot Glubman got drunk at a Sig Alph party and cried because he locked his keys in his dad's Cutlass, and the Cutlass was running. Gary's tears seemed different, though, holy in a way, like the tears you see at a funeral.

"He could see his kid's face, just six feet below him," said Gary. "But there was nothing he could do to help him. His eyes and mouth were, like, wide open, frozen like one of those guys in Pompeii."

"Oh, man."

"They say his lungs were full of water before the river patrol got to him."

Please… I shouted again at God, but only bubbles came out. I was no longer swimming like a normal human being, but like the last, pathetic creature on earth that missed the ark. If Milt had failed to get God's attention for lack of volume, that would certainly not be my mistake. I would bubble, and burble, and blubber so loudly at God that He would get sick of my commotion, and rush to my aid just to shut me up—even if it meant leaving Mr. Westminster to choke on his lamb.

Please, God! Please! Please! Please!

My head hit a rock, and the sound of it underwater was deep and full inside my lying cranium, and I saw stars and the face of a waterlogged boy.

Please, I whimpered.

"Relax," said God.

He said it just as loud and clear as that—like the collision of bone on boulder, under centuries of water poured out from His hand.

Water that fills.

Water that floods.

Water that blesses.

Water that buries the dead.

"Relax," God repeated. "Milt's boy has landed safely on My shore. Yours, on the other hand, has many more miles to paddle."

"Thank You, Sir," I burbled with a curtsy.

The next hard thing my head hit was the sharp stern-end of our canoe.

"I got your boat; you get your boy!" ordered Joe. We had worked our way into the shallows by that time, and when Joe flipped the canoe over, Wesley squinted up at the sun like a bear cub on a bright day.

"I lost my flip-flops!" he bellowed as I scooped him into my arms.

It was a weird first statement for someone who had come so close to death. I can only guess he was worried his mama might get on him if he didn't come home with all the things he had packed. Funny, that's the same thing I was worried about, too.

Mama, I'm sorry I lost my flip-flops.

Honey, I'm sorry I lost our son.

"We'll pick out some new flip-flops at Wal-Mart on the way home," I said, hugging Wesley tightly, so he could not know that some of the wetness on my face wasn't from the river.

And I wonder why tears do not come so easily to Wes at eighteen.

Squatting here in this hole, looking back at this memory of mine makes me wonder why I wasn't watching where I was going when we hit that insignificant twig. Pride is the only thing I can come up with. But that seems so ridiculous. Nobody is going to write on my grave someday: "He was a mighty fine paddler, God rest his soul." Nobody cares.

What I should have been doing was looking ahead at the rapids to come, scanning for hazards, picking my path.

Poor family fighters are guilty of this, too. Looking back, that is. It is one of my biggest mistakes when I fight with Cindy or the boys. We call this "backfield in motion" whenever we teach our conflict seminars. It is one of the most common errors in family fights, and it is so counterproductive that I will list it in "Will's Top Three Ways to Win a Fight…and Wind Up Losing," if you're into lists.

I am forty-six years old, and I have never told anyone what I am about to tell you in the next few sentences. Even my wife will be hearing this for the first time. After my sons hear it, they will verbally abuse me until I threaten to make them pay for their college educations.

Okay.

Deep breath.

All caution to the wind.

Here goes everything.

When I was in junior high I played for an eighth-grade football team called the Rebels. We absolutely stunk up the planet. We stunk it up so bad that once we lost a game 96–0. Ninety-six to nothing! Do you understand what I'm confessing here? We couldn't have lost any worse if we had spread out some of those kindergarten rest mats and taken naps on every play. It is virtually impossible to lose this badly in any sport, but we Rebels found a way.

There must have been a logical explanation.

I am wondering if any of us showed up for the game. Maybe we were buying sno-cones at the concession stand and got stuck in a long line behind a lady with thirty-five foster children. Maybe the kid at the counter didn't know how to make change. Maybe we were thinking about our name, the Rebels, and decided to take it seriously by rebelling against scoring. We couldn't have been that bad. Nobody is that bad.

Maybe we were just morons.

We had a lazy-eyed fullback named Danny, and he and I were friends. My dad said Danny's problem was anisometropic amblyopia, as if the medical name would help the rest of us feel more comfortable when our buddy's eye started wandering. As far as football players go we were all wastes of good gravity, but when it came to caring about each other we were pretty decent kids. Nobody ever made fun of Danny, probably because he was the only good athlete on the team. The problem with Danny was he couldn't run straight. He would start off going in motion, and then I guess his eye would freak out and he would veer toward the line before the ball was snapped, and the referees would throw their flags automatically.

"Backfield in motion!" they would holler, and we would be so mad we would all want to tackle the referee and tell him, "Danny can't be expected to run parallel to the line of scrimmage; he has a lazy eye, doofus! Why don't you get some glasses and fix your own lazy eye problems…or, like…maybe one of those seeing eye dogs, so you can see to make some…better calls…and stuff." We practiced getting angry like this on the sidelines, but we never actually said it to a referee. Who wants to draw more attention to himself when the score is 96–0?

Yep. We were morons.

Backfield in motion was our constant companion that season, slapped on us by referees every time a player going in motion ran toward the line before the ball was snapped. Danny had an excuse. The rest of us, however, did not.

In family fights, Backfield in Motion happens whenever one family member digs up something from the past to beat another family member. Put simply, things from our pasts need to stay in the backfield. Some of my most painful mistakes with Cindy and the boys have been the result of my bringing up their past to win a fight.

I want so badly for you to know that such behavior has no place in a family fight. It works well in a court of law, where real love does not exist, and the relationships between the attorneys and the people they question on the stand are tense and adversarial.

But attorneys are supposed to dig up the past. They get paid to be thorough, relentless, even brutal in their drive to expose weaknesses and sins. At the close of every legal case, there is a clear winner and a clear loser.

This is not so when the Backfield in Motion rule is violated in a family fight. There are no winners in this case—only losers.

Once, a long time ago, I forgave Wes for something he had done and honestly thought I had put it behind me. Tonight, however, when he repeated the same behavior, he hurt my feelings deeply, and, as I mentioned earlier, I found myself wanting to hurt him in return.

So I brought out the ancient, "forgiven" sin from storage and used it to strengthen my case against him. I remember Wes listening to me fairly well for a teenager being chewed out by his dad. He listened right up to the point I reminded him of his past offense. Then the light in his eyes snapped out, and he was looking at me with a look I had seen only one other time in life.

Where was that?

Where, oh where, had I seen that cold, cadaverous stare?

I think I know.

It was Milt's poor boy, looking back at me through miles and miles of water.

Someday Wes will get into his own canoe and paddle away from me for good; I know this. To be honest, he has been disappearing around the bend since he was sixteen. They say in time he'll come back, and that there's no telling what shape he'll be in when he does. He may be radiant with the news of an engagement, or a promotion, or a degree that is finally completed. Or he may come floating home on a board, in the backwash of bad living—waterlogged and weary, lungs plum full of the devil's elixir. I'd like to think I'll be ready for him either way, ready with open arms, just like I was when he came jabbering up out of the Buffalo.

I hope you will start making your fights present, my friend. In the *here* and in the *now.* Don't let your backfield be in motion any longer. Identify what has just hacked you off, and stick with it. If your loved one has offended you in similar fashion previously, deal with those incidents later. The goal is to advance, not go backward. You are a team. You must press on toward the goal line. You are fellow travelers in the same canoe, and the rapids ahead may require all of you to paddle. People who stand up in canoes and taunt water are just weird.

Forget the rapids behind.

God Thoughts

THE GREAT EGGPLANT REBELLION

We had no black sheep in our family, only a speckled one: my younger sister Charlotte.

Named after the cigar-smoking, whiskey-drinking favorite grandma of mine, Charlotte was mostly a good child—until things didn't go her way; then she would show her speckles. My most speckled memory of Charlotte happened on the one and only night our mother served eggplant.

I remember Mom setting it down in the middle of the table, and all of us just looking at it. Even Dad stared blankly at the steaming, purple mass. After a moment, he reached for it with his fork and knife and, as if to comfort himself with activity, began to carve it.

"It looks delicious," said my older sister, Claudia, whom we sometimes called Mary Poppins. (Her hair could be on fire and she would probably write a song about it.)

Jeannette, the youngest, was off the hook, of course. Too old for baby food, but too young to be force-fed eggplant, she was already working on a plateful of cut-up wienies when the meal began.

Then there was Charlotte.

"I'm not eating it," she declared flatly.

"Me neither," I chimed in.

We both looked at Dad to see if he would complete our quorum.

"You'll have it for breakfast," he warned without flinching.

Mary Poppins lifted a slice from the platter and put it on

her plate. "I can't wait to try it," she said cheerily. I half expected to see a bluebird tie a ribbon around her fork and lift it to her mouth. In the kitchen, Mom was taking off her apron and pouring glasses of milk for the family.

Charlotte and I folded our arms and sat back in our chairs.

"Suit yourselves," said Dad. "But both of you will have to eat one slice of eggplant before you do anything else."

The Great Eggplant Rebellion had begun.

According to historians, since 3500 B.C. the earth has experienced only 292 years without any type of warfare. It is also a little-known fact that those were the same years when all the eggplant farmers went on strike…and everyone just ate candy…and that is the closest we have ever come to world peace.

Whether or not we believed Dad when he told us that our lives as we knew them would be put on hold until we had eaten our portion of eggplant is up for grabs. All I know is that the next thing Charlotte did was stand up from the table and declare that not only was she boycotting eggplant…she was now officially running away.

I was mortified.

Dad, on the other hand, took Charlotte's resignation from the family in stride.

"I'll help you pack your bags," he said.

"Fine," said Charlotte.

"I don't think this is a good idea," I said.

"Well, I don't know why not," said Dad, turning toward me. "You were perfectly happy to support this rebellion a moment ago. Where's your courage now, soldier?"

"Yeah! Where's your courage?" said Charlotte. She had no idea Dad had already won the battle of the emotions and had turned his attention to the battle of the mind.

"Now, I think the best thing for each of you to do is to pack a little suitcase with plenty of clothes for a week."

"A week?" I said.

"Well, a person can't run away properly unless he goes for a minimum of seven days—can he?"

"But we'll get hungry," I said, injecting reason into the conversation.

"Nonsense—I'll make sure we fix up a picnic basket, loaded to the top with whatever we can find in the refrigerator. Of course, it will be one more thing for you to carry; but it won't be long before you both have secured good jobs and are able to buy a car."

"Dad, we aren't even ten yet."

"Hmm. You've got a point there, son. Oh, well—I suppose toting heavy suitcases and picnic baskets for six or seven years won't be all that bad. Just think of all the muscle you'll build. All right. Is everybody ready?"

"Yes!" said Charlotte.

"No!" said I.

"Good," said Dad. "Let's forget about this silly old eggplant and go pack."

When I was a boy, something about the Parable of the Prodigal Son touched me deeply. For a long time I thought it was the happy ending that attracted me. But after thinking about it for a while I realized my head was stuffed with stories of happy endings—of glass slippers that fit, and wooden puppets that attained boyhood, and little piggies that went "wee, wee, wee" all the way home. None of them stood with special meaning above the others; they were a dime a dozen. I determined it had to be something else.

And then I hit upon it one day in college, when I was having a quiet time. The father himself was the reason I liked the story. I liked him whether his boy came home or not. He was compassionate, yet respectable—other-centered, yet self-secure. He loved his boy, which was evidenced by the fact he was watching like a lighthouse when his boy returned. But he also respected himself enough not to go all to pieces when the prodigal took his inheritance and left. He didn't beg him to stay, or chain him to the porch, or offer some kind of bribe. A part of me always wondered if the father might have even helped the prodigal pack his bags.

But the Bible is silent on this matter.

We packed our belongings in a blur of instructions for the road—with Charlotte taking notes from Dad on things like locating an apartment, preparing for an interview, and protecting oneself against used-car salesmen. Meanwhile, I threw up in my suitcase.

We said our good-byes at the front door. At this point, even Mary Poppins was having a hard time putting on a happy face. “Are you sure you want to go through with this?” she asked.

“It’s not too late to change your mind,” said Dad.

I started to pipe up, but Charlotte pinched the skin just above my hip and gave it a good twist.

“Our minds are made up,” she said.

“Okay,” said Dad, “but I owe you one last bit of advice.”

Something in the way he said this made even Charlotte stop to listen.

“When you get to the end of the block, it would probably be wise to walk on the opposite side of the street,” he said.

“Why?” asked Charlotte.

“Well…because of the witch, of course.”

“What witch?”

“The one from *The Wizard of Oz*. You didn’t suspect she’d stay in movies forever, did you? She retired and moved to our neighborhood.”

Charlotte looked suspiciously at Dad, and I could tell she was cracking. We had just recently watched *The Wizard of Oz* as a family, and already both she and I had been terrorized by it in our dreams.

“Which house is hers?” she asked.

“She bought the Yinger place when they moved out last month. Anyway, be quiet when you walk by—she’s not too fond of children and all their noise.”

★ ★ ★

The pigpen must have been a wretched place for the prodigal son—chock-full of filth and smells and the witches of his childhood. It is a terrifying thing to be away from home before you are ready.

With suitcases and picnic basket in hand, Charlotte and I walked out the door, across the porch, down the stairs, and onto the lawn where a golden rectangle of light from the house bounced out into the shadows and disappeared.

"More light!" demanded Charlotte.

"That's all there is," replied Dad. "Be careful of the witch."

"We'll kill the old witch," muttered Charlotte, but I could tell her heart wasn't in it as much as it had been five minutes before.

Still, her pride was strong, so off we went.

We made it past the Emmills' house, which was the house next door to ours…but that depleted most of our courage. Twenty paces onto the Robertsons' property, our march slowed to a crawl.

"I don't much feel like fighting witches, anyway," said Charlotte.

"Me neither," I agreed. "We'd have licked her, though."

"Oh, yeah. We'd have licked her good."

"Wanna go home?"

"Do you?"

"Maybe."

"Char?"

"What?"

"You think he'll make us eat the eggplant?"

I think the prodigal's heart stopped when he saw his father running toward him.

He probably hadn't seen his dad run in years—maybe never. Most kids don't get to see their dads run. They only see them with slacks on, walking out the door for the office.

I saw my dad run once. A bunch of the neighborhood kids were playing a game of tag in our backyard, and he was "it." It was pretty weird at first; but then I thought it was cool. I can only imagine how it would feel to have him running toward me, coming from a very long way off, with his knees high and his arms pumping, coming as if I were the last drink of water on the planet—and he hadn't had a sip in years.

To our knowledge, the prodigal's father never again brought up the subject of his son's sins in the far-off country. There were no reminders of the emotional stress he had caused, no financial ledgers flung in his face as evidence of how he had bankrupted the family's net worth. Instead, his father threw him the biggest, fattest, most ridiculously extravagant party possible, and all the neighbors were invited.

Our Father in heaven loves the wanderers and the squanderers. That's why He sent His Son down into the pigpen, to suffer the smells with us and to be treated like filth on our behalf. This makes it possible for us to go home to Him, possible for us to live with the knowledge that Backfield in Motion will never be part of His household. For He has set our sins as far as the east is from the west, a fact that makes our heavenly home all the more desirable. And after all, home should be the easiest place in the universe for a child to return to.

Is your home like this?

Charlotte and I came home five minutes after we left—though it felt like we had been prodigals in a far-off country for a lifetime. True to his word, Dad made us eat our one slice of eggplant, but we never had eggplant again in our household. And I have never served it to my children, either. In fact, it is as if *all* eggplants became extinct that night; forty years later I don't even notice them in stores.

Later when Dad was tucking me into bed, I recall his warm arm across my chest as he said my prayers with me:

Now I lay me down to sleep,
Still picking eggplant from my teeth.
If I should die before I wake,
I pray in heaven they serve steak.

Sumpin's Burning

UNNECESSARY ROUGHNESS

"Some men have a way with words—some men don't."
I saw this once on a billboard for domestic violence.
Beneath it was a woman with a black eye.
I think we are living on a haunted planet.

There are two kinds of law in the Ozarks.

There's the law of the land, and then there's the law that rests deep in the hollows, down where the trolls roast mushrooms over open fires and the smoke is sweet and blue.

I once bought a house under this second category of the law. Actually, I didn't buy it; I squatted in it. I backed a truck the size of the *Santa Maria* up the driveway and moved all my possessions inside *before* I talked to the bank about a loan. I did everything but drive my sword in the front lawn and claim it for the mother country. And I did all this on the advice of my realtor—a character by the name of Rex, who has sold homes to half the trolls in southern Missouri.

"This seems a little backward," I confided to Rex as I was hooking up my refrigerator and he was unpacking his brain of everything he knew about bass fishing.

"Boy, the bank is gonna love you," Rex assured me.

"Yes, but what if the bank were to stop by tonight and find me living in this house? That would be a little awkward, don't you think?"

"Quit yer worryin', boy."

"What if the *owner* came by?"

"Lookit—some of the finest people I know have bought their first homes in exactly the same way."

"But this is my fourth home, and none of the others have been remotely like this."

Rex dismissed me with the wave of a hand and sailed off into a discourse on the speckled trout. The next day I went to talk with a loan officer, and everything went just as Rex had prophesied. The officer told me he had once been a squatter, too, in a trailer over near Blue Eye—where the elves and the satyrs run a small but respectable real estate company. I have never gotten used to the Ozarks…

Which is why I'm still here.

I had my first real brush with Ozark law two years later, when I committed a felony and didn't even know it. "Class D felony" is the name attached to thefts over the amount of $250. If you are thinking of stealing things, then it is a good idea not to exceed this amount. In my case, I hadn't stolen anything—and I still got blamed for it.

"You Will Cunningham?" asked the police officer one fine Friday in June.

"Yes, sir, that would be me."

We were standing in the parking lot of the residential treatment center where I used to work—a place for troubled teens and white-collar rebels who have worn out their welcome in their parents' homes. Since visits from the police were not uncommon at the center, I thought the officer was there on behalf of one of our residents. You can imagine my shock when he showed me the warrant for my own arrest and began to read my rights.

"What did I do?" I interrupted.

"I don't rightly know, son, but it must have been somethin', 'cause I got this here warrant."

I scrolled back in my mind, trying to recall recent acts of deviance. Suddenly it dawned on me. "This wouldn't have anything to do with an auto dealership, would it?"

The officer looked down at the warrant, then back up with a nod. "Well, yes it does...says here you cancelled a check."

I held out my hands.

"What?" asked the officer.

"I thought you'd want to cuff me."

"Son, this ain't New York City."

Now, the auto dealership that filed the charges shall remain nameless, since I do not wish any ill will to come upon that establishment. But believe me when I tell you I will ride a burro before I buy their brand of vehicle again. This is not a bitter resolve—just a regular one. How else should I respond toward the company who ruined my engine on the day I was going to visit my dying dad in the hospital? I didn't have to like it then. And I don't have to like it now.

"Am I going to spend time in jail?" I asked the officer.

"Depends on if you can post bail, son," he replied.

"How much would that be?"

"Two thousand dollars."

Reality settled around my shoulders like a heavy yoke.

"I'll need to stop by my home to get our checkbook," I said, knowing full well we didn't have that kind of money in our account. I mostly just wanted to say good-bye to Cindy, in case we wouldn't be seeing each other for a while.

"I'll follow you in my car," said the officer.

All the way home I heard the trolls laughing their belly laughter down in the caves and crevices—yukking up a storm about the homespun justice that passes for law in these hills. When I came in the back door, Cindy was doing dishes and was surprised to see me home early. Now, I didn't want to scare her, but I also didn't want her to be wondering where I was come suppertime—so I resolved to tell the whole truth and to tell it quickly.

"Remember that brake job I had done on my car last December?" I began.

"I think so."

"Do you also remember how unhappy I was with it? And how after I picked the car up and got about thirty miles down the road, the transmission went out? And how I told the dealership I was tired of taking my car in for minor problems, and receiving it back with major problems...and how I also told them I thought they needed to reimburse me for a new transmission...and how they said no...and how I finally just cancelled the check I had written for the brake job? Do you remember all of that?"

"I think so."

"Good—because I'm going to need the checkbook again."

"What for?"

"I have to go to jail."

"That's nice, dear."

"Okay. Tell the boys I'll write soon."

Cindy gave me a kiss and went back to doing dishes, and I had neither the guts nor the time to tell her I wasn't joking.

★ ★ ★

There are hidden costs to a good sense of humor.

At the Forsyth jail I met Sheriff Jenkins—a tall and lank individual, with hardly enough lawman to fill his own uniform. I liked him immediately—in fact, I voted for him in the next election.

"What seems to be the problem?" he asked as I stood with the policeman in front of his desk. I remember thinking he sounded more like a country doctor than a sheriff.

"Class D felony," said the policeman, handing the sheriff my warrant.

Sheriff Jenkins gave me the once-over.

"Well, well, well. I ain't seen you in here before—you don't look the type to commit a felony. What's a good kid like you doing in a place like this?"

"I, uh, cancelled a check to a dealership," I replied.

Sheriff Jenkins scanned the warrant. "You pulled stunts like this before?"

"No sir."

"You a married man?"

"Yes sir."

"Got young 'uns?"

"Yes sir—two."

"Pay your taxes?"

"Every year."

Sheriff Jenkins tossed the warrant on his desk and sat back in his chair. "Lemme tell ya, kid, this place is full of roughnecks—and you don't look like one of 'em. If I was to put you in here, it would be the worst experience of your young life. Like

I said, you look like a good kid; why don't you head on back to that dealership and pay 'em what you owe 'em? After that you can hustle back here and settle your court fees. Then you're free to go."

"No kidding, sir?"

"No kiddin'.'"

"You mean I'm free to go—like, right now? With no bond?"

"That's what I said, kid. Hurry up or I might decide to change my mind."

I started to walk out to my car, but something inside me was too curious.

"Say, sheriff," I said, returning to his desk. "I don't mean to take up more of your time, but let's pretend you didn't think I was such a good person, and you decided to go ahead and put me in jail. What cell would I have been in?"

"That's easy," said the sheriff, pointing to a small bank of monitors on the wall behind him. He paused on one in particular that showed a lone prisoner in a leather jacket, talking to someone on the phone. "First of all, I would never in a million years put you in a cell with this guy."

"Why not?" I asked.

"Too dangerous."

"What's he in for?"

The sheriff scratched his head. "Officer from Kissee Mills says he killed a fella last night over a game of pool. Says he beat him to death with a pool stick—blood everywhere. He's making a call to his lawyer, I think. Nah, I probably wouldn't put you in a cell with him."

"Thanks. So, where would you have put me?"

"I'da put you over here with these yahoos," said the sheriff, pointing to a monitor that showed six guys playing cards around a makeshift table. "Bunch of the town drunks—pretty good fellas when they're sober, though. They wouldn'ta gave you too hard a time."

"Well, thanks, sheriff," I said, shaking his hand. "I'm sorry I can't repay you."

"Vote," said the sheriff. "That'll be payment enough."

A moment later I was out in the sunshine a free man, driving to the dealership to pay my bill.

If at that moment I could have seen into my heart, through the wall of my chest and rib cage and all the other stuff in there, I would have seen a heart split clean down the middle on the topics of love and forgiveness.

On the one side, my heart was as bright and cheery as the day outside my car window. But on the other, it was a chunk of coal.

And that's the side that worried me.

Sometimes people live with anger so long in their lives it calcifies into black, useless chunks. Maybe the chunks are there because people are still mad at their dad for not fishing with them enough. Maybe their dad fished with them, but he also fondled them. Maybe it was mom they're mad at…or a nasty, drunk uncle…or a cute cousin who always seemed to make the cheerleading squad with ease. Maybe they're full of chunks because they can't forgive a car dealership.

The next morning, I was drinking orange juice and having my quiet time on the front porch when a verse in Matthew 5 caught my attention.

> "You have heard that it was said to the people long ago, 'Do not murder, and anyone who murders will

> be subject to judgment.' But I tell you that anyone who is angry with his brother will be subject to judgment. Again, anyone who says to his brother, 'Raca,' is answerable to the Sanhedrin. But anyone who says, 'You fool!' will be in danger of the fire of hell."

I remember thinking at that moment that God was trying to tell me something—that He was chiseling away at the hard, black part of my heart like a sweat-glistened construction worker with a jackhammer.

"That Jesus," I laughed to myself, "always shaking things up to get the attention of the Pharisees." Then I went inside to shave and start my day.

As I passed the dining room table I saw the newspaper headline:

FORSYTH JAIL BURNS TO THE GROUND;
THREE PRISONERS DIE OF SMOKE INHALATION

Anger is the most delicate of all human emotions. I know this sounds goofy, but it's true.

The best way I know how to explain it is by reminding you of one of those old episodes of *Mission: Impossible* where the secret agent has to handle a vial of nitroglycerin, knowing that one false move will cause it to explode. Anger is like nitroglycerin—very delicate and unpredictable. Handled carelessly, it can wreak havoc.

I used to think the Bible contradicted itself when I compared Jesus' words about anger in Matthew 5 to Paul's words in Ephesians 4:26, "Be angry, and yet do not sin" (NASB). Now I believe that Paul was making two points, and that both of them were in agreement with Jesus.

On the one hand, he was saying, "When you get mad, do it in the sinless way—not the sinful way." This is encouraging to me, because it makes me think that even someone like me, someone who loses his temper now and then, might still have a chance of getting it right someday.

Just as we learned in the chapter on Offsides that there are right and wrong times for fighting, so we see here that there are right and wrongs *ways* to get angry. Right ways bring reward. Wrong ways are unnecessary and rough.

The other thing Paul was saying can only be understood if we reverse Ephesians 4:26, rendering its antithesis, *"Refuse to be angry, and wind up sinning."* Here we're reminded of the nitroglycerin thing again, and we become aware that anger held inward is extremely dangerous; one jiggle too many and we have carnage on our hands, like Columbine. One jiggle too few and we have depression, and ultimately suicide.

I try to keep short accounts of my anger now, kind of like regularly balancing a checkbook. When in balance, the potential for conflict is so much less.

The character of anger is tenuous. It is to be both feared and valued, loathed and desired, handled like a ticking bomb and spent wisely like one's paycheck.

There is nothing like the death of one man to get the second man thinking about his life.

★ ★ ★

The news of the Forsyth jail fire was sobering for me, and I lived with it quietly until I finally just had to tell Cindy the truth about my whereabouts that day. Right in the middle of my confession Cindy's face turned pale, and she put her hands to her mouth as if to stop the unspeakable thing she was about to say.

"If Sheriff Jenkins hadn't been so kind to you, you'd have been in there when the fire started. You'd have..."

She never finished the sentence, but I always knew she understood the weight of the grudge that almost burned our family to the ground.

★ ★ ★

Fire is no respecter of persons. Its chief aim is to reduce everything to ash, whether noble or ignoble. It doesn't care whether you have murdered a man with a pool stick, or silently hated him for wrecking your engine. In the end, fire always gets its man.

I once saw Jim McMahon of the defending Super Bowl Champion Chicago Bears get clobbered in a game. It was a Packer defensive lineman who did the damage. He charged into the Bear backfield, picked up McMahon and body-slammed him to the turf long after the whistle had blown to end the play. The Packer was fined severely, but that was no consolation for McMahon, who was sidelined with an injured shoulder for the rest of the 1986 season.

That was one of the most flagrant Unnecessary Roughness violations to mar professional football in years—so flagrant that it got the attention of team league officials and led to game-changing regulations concerning the protection of quarterbacks. Those new regulations are still adhered to today in 2006.

But far more tragic are the personal attacks and character assassinations that embitter many family fights. Unnecessary Roughness of the verbal or physical kind is no stranger to many families, and it hurts deeper and longer than the hardest body slams in the NFL.

Some of you are downright mean when you get angry. I don't know which ones you are, but I can guess you didn't like reading the previous sentence. Nobody likes being told he has a temper—especially those who really do. Nevertheless, if this is true of you, then it's high time someone brought it to your attention.

The two most common ways to be unnecessarily rough with your spouse:

1. *words* that hurt
2. *hands* that hurt

"Hey, Dumbo! You look like a taxi going down the street with your doors open." As a child, I heard words like these regarding my big ears. Although my child-size head eventually caught up with my adult-size ears, I carried the scars of unnecessary roughness for many years. I was thirty years old before I felt comfortable with a haircut that showed the slightest part of the lobe.

It's a great temptation to violate the Unnecessary Roughness rule when we fight. Our words have the power to stop a person dead in his tracks. But what's the *real* reason we do it? Are our vocabularies so narrow that we must resort to name-calling, swearing, or ridiculing?

No, we use rough words in hopes of winning a conflict—which, as I have already said, is an empty victory anyway. If we set out to win a family fight, we will always lose in the long run. And the loss will be all the more tragic if we use Unnecessary Roughness.

Rough words are not the only way someone can burn his family to the ground. Rough hands can start a fire, too.

Sometimes physical roughness invades a marriage or family. This is particularly destructive because the victim of such abuse feels threatened at the most basic level of his or her security. Losing one's sense of significance is one thing, but losing one's sense of safety, especially in the very place where one should feel most safe, is devastating.

Years ago I met with a woman named Rhonda and her son, Bobby. I knew from the moment she approached my secretary's desk and looked around for assistance that the two of them were members of the walking wounded. Bobby clung tightly to his mother's tattered overcoat, his smaller-than-average four-year-old body pressed against her leg as if he would have loved nothing more than to be absorbed by her—and hidden from the world.

"Please come in," I said. Rhonda and Bobby positioned themselves on the couch. Rhonda sat with her arms folded and her jaw set. When I offered to let Bobby sit on my lap during our conversation, as I often do with young children, he declined. Without taking his eyes from me, he leaned his head against his mother's side and assumed a silent, watchful manner.

"He's just shy," his mother offered. "I was like that, too, when I was his age."

Shy was not the word I would have picked to describe Bobby.

"We're here because we're leaving, and I was told you could help us find a place to go," Rhonda continued. "We've checked some shelters, but they all say they're full and that we need to be in a life-threatening situation before they'll take us."

Rhonda reached up with her right hand and smoothed back her hair. I saw a small bruise on her temple. I glanced at Bobby, noticing for the first time similar signs of abuse.

Rhonda said her husband's attacks had been reported by neighbors, but nothing was ever done about it. She told of an occasion when her husband punished Bobby for letting the dog out of their yard. "He made Bobby bend down and kiss his shoe, then he kicked him." She said another neighbor saw the incident and telephoned authorities—but again no action was taken.

"Nine years is enough," she said. "We aren't going back."

"You won't have to go back," I assured Rhonda, but I had little else to say. The damage had been done.

Because the shelters couldn't take them, we arranged for Rhonda and Bobby to stay with a family in our church. I watched as they left that day, Rhonda's torn coat flapping in the August wind and Bobby's little body blending into hers.

What will become of them? I wondered. *Where will Rhonda be ten years from now? What type of man will Bobby grow up to be?*

Unnecessary Roughness of verbal or physical nature is a major roadblock to conflict resolution. It is one of the hardest roadblocks to overcome because of its lasting scars. Even if you determine never to be unnecessarily rough with your spouse or children again, you must be prepared to accept the fact that your poor track record will follow you for quite some time. Trust broken through abuse is not easily restored.

The fire of Unnecessary Roughness is rolling across our countryside, burning up the tender blades of relationships, taking down households like stacks of kindling. Such fire starts in one's heart, then spreads to one's mouth and one's hands. And the only way it can be stopped is with water—lots of it.

Holy Spirit, rain your healing water down upon our homes.

Quench our anger.

Soothe our wounds.

TENDER AS HELL

I want you to imagine for a moment the hands and mouth of the devil, starting with his hands.

I bet they are smooth to the eye and rough to the touch—pampered with idleness, but exposed to centuries of cold so deep it feels like fire. If the devil shook hands with you, you would be both flattered and lacerated at the same time. His children flinch whenever he pats their heads. His wife hates to slow dance. I cannot imagine anything more frightening than the devil's hands—unless it is his mouth.

The devil's mouth is a perpetual grin—never truly smiling when he makes love to his wife, and never truly frowning when he abuses her. His rotten teeth are a thin shield for his rotten breath. He eats with all the courtesy of Time, and drinks like a sewer drain.

But by far the most distinguishing and horrifying feature of the devil's mouth is the voice it broadcasts. It is the promise of goodness with no follow-through...beauty with the mute button on...*Ave Maria* through a megaphone.

It strikes me as important that the Bible mentions God's hands or His mouth in nearly every book. He is a constant source of provision and encouragement to those who love Him—and even to those who don't.

I wonder how my own hands and mouth will be remembered.

Will they remind my heirs of God's goodness and cheer?

Or will they be a legacy of hell's tenderness?

Harvey

TOO MANY PLAYERS ON THE FIELD

If I'd have known my future father-in-law was a twenty-five-year Navy man, I don't think I'd have worn the jeans with the holes in the rear on the day we first met.

You can choose a lot of things in life, but in-laws aren't one of them. We don't choose in-laws; we inherit them in the same way we inherit the smell of a car we buy. My father-in-law has always had a "new car" smell about him, like one of those zippy little roadsters. But in the twenty-five years I've known him, I've never seen him get pushed around by a larger model. Harvey pretty much rules the road.

Back on the first page of this book I mentioned that I'm about as prepared for life as a snowman in July, and I hoped you would understand the metaphor. If you didn't, maybe the following story will clear things up for you. Here is what happened on the day I drove four hundred miles to see what Harvey-the-Eagle-Scout-and-twenty-five-year-Navy-man would say if I wanted to take his daughter away from him and marry her.

It was a hundred and one on a dog's belly the morning I left Oklahoma City in my Buick Special. "Old Gold" was the name I had given her in an attempt to conjure up images of mysterious, hidden value. But every time I said the words, I knew they were ordinary veneer for a piece of junk.

I took little with me for my journey, which is the same as saying I took everything I owned—my car, my carcass, and a jar of pennies I'd been collecting since I started receiving allowance in the first grade. I figured it would come in handy on my trek to Kansas City. As it turned out, this was the only smart thing I did that day.

At noon it was a hundred and four, and I had made it all the way to the Flint Hills. If you have never driven across this moonlike landscape, I suggest you do it at nighttime, preferably in the dead of January with an ice storm bearing down on you. That way you won't have to see a thing, and the roads will still be bone dry—because a glacier could fall from the sky, and it would melt before it reached the ground; it is so unbearably hot in the Flint Hills.

At one-thirty I saw a tiny speck in my rearview mirror, and I watched it grow and grow, until the speck became a black Dodge Challenger with a Boss 302 engine.

Mother of pearl! I said to myself, slowing down to gawk. *That's one fine vehicle behind me...cruising along at seventy-five...with its top down...and its radio blaring...and its front bumper just two inches from my rear bumper...and its driver expressing his undying love for me with indisputable hand signals.*

"Get off the road," the driver shouted, as he blew past me in a blur.

"I'll show you 'get off the road,'" I muttered, romping on Old Gold's gas pedal to see what she would do.

Now I don't know what I expected would happen when I

floored a car that was fifteen years old, but I suppose I hoped Old Gold would reach down inside herself and summon the ancient horsepower to catch up with the Challenger. This, however, was a hope deferred—for no sooner had I pushed the pedal to the metal than Old Gold's engine overheated and she coasted to the shoulder of the road. There was not another car on the moon for miles that day.

I looked at my watch, and noted the five o'clock dinner engagement I had with Cindy's parents was barely three hours away. For the next hour I read my Bible, made animals out of the sparse clouds, did push-ups, and tried to start my car. Finally at three-thirty Old Gold coughed once and rattled back to life. I turned the air conditioner off to keep from overheating again, and away I went with renewed vigor.

In five minutes the vigor was gone, and in it place was the wretched heat.

It is important to remember when you go a-wandering across this great land we call America that you sometimes encounter strange and unexpected roadblocks known as "tolls." This is something the Snowman had not remembered. In fact, he had never paid a toll before and was surprised when a man in a little outhouse told him he owed three dollars for using the highway. So, melting away to pungent rivulets on his black leather seat, the Snowman rolled pennies to pay the toll.

"One hundred and twenty…one hundred and twenty-one…one hundred and twenty-two…"

There were three tolls along that stretch of highway—each requiring three hundred more pennies for the great state of Kansas, each siphoning off a gallon of sweat from the Snowman's body, each using up precious minutes in the Snowman's mad race to meet a man who was his polar opposite.

There was nothing else that could go wrong, except maybe to…

With a shudder, Old Gold died about a rock's throw from a service station; she had run out of gas. The Snowman did not say any bad words—mostly because he was dehydrated and delirious and was having trouble formulating thoughts, much less syllables, as he pushed his car to the station and fell down in a puddle of misery and bumper shade. After a while he figured he ought to count his pennies and buy some gas; but when he did, the Snowman discovered he did not even have enough money left for one gallon.

So the Snowman decided to make a phone call, and he glommed into the service station to inquire as to the whereabouts of a phone.

"Phone's out back," said the friendly man at the counter.

The Snowman did not even say "thank you" to the friendly man, because his lips had melted off in the heat. He just glommed around the building and found the phone just as the man had said, except that he had not mentioned anything about the wide expanse of sundress that would be talking on it—and talking, and talking, and talking, and talking.

The Snowman sank down in the shadow of the sundress, and he waited, and waited, and waited, and melted, and melted, and melted. And the sundress talked, and talked, and talked, and talked—and when the talking, and waiting, and melting had all blended together into what appeared to the Snowman to be a great, big, indistinguishable mass of burbled blah, the Snowman lapsed into a dream.

He dreamed of a sleek blue Cadillac with a naval emblem on the driver's door, pulling up to where he lay evaporating. Out of the car stepped a sharply dressed man.

"Harvey Ray—pleased to meet you," said the man, extending his hand.

The Snowman in a daze tried to stand to his feet, but he collapsed with an *oof* and shook Mr. Ray's hand from a sitting position.

"Pleeshzz to burble dooba meetcha," said the Snowman, too weak to care that every last shred of his oratory skills had vanished with the thaw.

"It's unfortunate that you've run out of gas, son. Don't you have any money?"

The Snowman opened his sweaty palm, and seventeen copper coins grinned up at his future father-in-law.

"Well now, that is unfortunate…that's very unfortunate indeed. It never pays to be unprepared. Have I mentioned that before I reached the age of seventeen, I earned my Eagle Scout?"

The Snowman shook his watery head—he shook it long and hard, each shake in honor of all the snow-headed things he had done throughout life that had earned him nothing save this hot pavement.

"We better get you into the air-conditioning," said Harvey, taking the Snowman by his sweaty sleeve and leading him to the car.

The last thing the Snowman remembered from that dream was sinking back into the cool leather seats of the sharply dressed man's car and wondering how long it would take for him to get his Eagle Scout.

With minimal exaggeration, this is pretty much how things went on the day I went to discuss marriage with my future father-in-law. Harvey paid for my gas and I followed him to

Kansas City, wondering all the way what kind of impression I had made on him.

Actually, I had already met him before in the hospital; so if you keep in mind that my first impression on Harvey had been made three months earlier, when he received the news that I was the person driving on the morning his daughter was nearly killed, you can understand why my asking his permission for Cindy's hand in marriage was beginning to seem more like a request to abduct her.

Why he ever gave consent is beyond me.

The only reason it is important for you to know all of this is because there are certain people in the world who you may be tempted at times to drag into your fights. The list includes: in-laws, siblings, best friends, pastors, marriage counselors, camp directors, and your own children. Harvey has made it a time or two into the Cunningham family fights, as have my mother and several of our friends. In each case, Cindy and I have been guilty of "too many players on the field."

In every sport there are limits on the number of participants who can play at one time. When this rule is broken, it is generally because of some oversight. But in a marital conflict, where the number of players should be limited to two, the violation of Too Many Players on the Field is rarely an oversight; it is a deliberate choice of the spouse who seeks to strengthen his or her case against the other spouse. This is always unfair, and there is never any place for it in a family fight.

Do you have a parent, friend, or sibling to whose wisdom or behaviors you occasionally refer in order to win points in a fight? If so, consider what this may be doing to your relationship. What if every time I made a Snowman-ish decision that differed from the way Harvey would have done things, Cindy came back with, "That's not how Dad does it"? Would you think that was fair? Of course you wouldn't. Nobody in his logical mind thinks this way. And yet…marriages all over the world are plagued with Too Many Players on the Field.

Before marrying each other, a man and woman should agree to establish their own traditions, plan their own vacations, choose their own place of worship, make their own decisions regarding the discipline of children, and so forth. Every couple is like a brand-new country, a baby nation that has sprung from the mother countries of two other nations.

Figuratively speaking, one spouse came from France and the other Spain. In France, we can assume that French was always spoken—but probably not a lick of Spanish. In Spain, we can assume the opposite was true. For a new marriage to work, new languages must be invented. Husbands or wives who resist developing "Spench" or "Franish"—the amalgamation of two distinct languages—are the ones who usually violate Too Many Players on the Field.

Each new couple should choose to resolve their conflicts without dragging their parents or anybody else into the issue. If you reach an impasse, seek the counsel of a pastor or marital counselor.

Here are three common ways people break the rule of Too Many Players on the Field:

1. They appeal to parental opinions or preferences to support their side in a conflict.
2. They give in to the temptation to share the "dirty laundry" with an outsider, such as a parent or a friend.

3. They draw their own children into the middle of a spousal conflict in an effort to "beat" the other person.

Recently I spoke with a man who was going through a painful divorce. Because I knew both him and his wife, I was even more saddened by the news of their upcoming split. Even sadder was the fact that their two-year-old daughter was being dragged into their battle. The wife was insisting on sole custody of their child as the only option in their divorce agreement, and was refusing to let her husband see the child. "I can hardly believe my wife would be this vindictive," he told me. "I feel she is just trying to pay me back for all her past hurts, and she's doing it by putting our daughter between the two of us."

Broken marriages are always devastating, but when children are used as weapons in the process, it's the worst case of Too Many Players on the Field. Leave outsiders where they belong...on the outside.

I have heard many tales of horrific in-laws; and after hearing them, I am doubly thankful for the in-laws God has given me. But in spite of how wonderful our parents are, Cindy and I left twenty-five years ago to start our own home, our own country. If we want to eat chocolate cake for breakfast every morning, or answer our phones in a Swedish accent, or roll pennies to pay tolls for the rest of our lives, it is our country's prerogative to do so.

Mmm.

I like that chocolate cake idea.

CLEAVAGE

There's a lot of talk nowadays about the "new cleavage."

In fact, just this morning I think I saw it. Cindy and I were at a café eating Danish and sipping coffee. "Would you mind getting me a napkin?" Cindy asked.

"One napkin for the lady coming right up," I said.

At the counter where the napkins are found, a small knot of humanity had gotten tangled in their quest for silverware and lemon wedges, and was trying politely to disentangle itself. All of sudden, someone dropped a tray and oatmeal exploded everywhere. In the midst of it all, a college girl bent over to pick up the pieces; and where her blouse took leave of her britches I was introduced to the "new cleavage."

"Look, Mommy," said an astute five-year-old boy, "that girl's bottom looks like a chest."

The boy's mother turned instantly into a mute lump of stone, so he looked at me for a response.

"Why, yes it does," I said, trying without success not to laugh. "And if her mommy bought her shirts that weren't too little and pants that weren't too low, she could keep her bottom to herself—but then, you and I would have never met each other, would we?"

The boy smiled and we shook hands, and as we were parting ways I leaned close to him, waved a butter knife in front of his eyes, made a little clicking noise, and said, "You will forget everything you have just seen until you are twenty-five and at the altar getting married. Then it will all come back to you like magic, and you will thank me for it."

"Cool," said the boy.

"Yeah, really cool."

Someday my five-year-old friend *will* grow up, just as I prophesied.

He will stand at the altar and tremble like the rest of us who have made the leap across the chasm of aloneness. As he says, "I do," he will wonder if he'll be able to keep his word. And as he kisses his bride, he will wonder if she'll be able to love him once she really gets to know him.

Then my new friend will turn his wife toward the crowd, and the preacher will pronounce them Mr. and Mrs. So-and-So, and the congregation will burst into applause as they start down the aisle. But just as they reach the bottom of the stairs, they will look at their parents and a knowing glance will pass between them.

"This is it," the glance will say. "The moment we've dreamed and prepared for—the emptying out of one nest and the filling of another. The decline of one nation, and the birth of another."

God's plan has always included this component—cleavage, that is. Matthew 19:5 states it clearly when Jesus says, "For this reason a man will leave his father and mother and *cleave* to his wife, and the two will become one flesh."

As my friend and I learned at the café, some cleavage is counterfeit, contrived, and inappropriate. I think this kind of cleavage is most often seen in couples that have retained the past at the expense of the present and the future. This is the wife who doesn't want to leave France, or the husband who is so entrenched in Spain he can't even fathom a move. They cling to old traditions from their families of origin, flatly refusing to develop traditions of their own. They vacation at the same spots, and watch the same TV shows their parents watched. Sunday is pork tenderloin and NFL football, and thou shalt not deviate!

Following traditions from one's family of origin is not necessarily bad, unless it serves to keep people from growing up and branching out. God loves the formation of *new* countries—new territories with the potential of being claimed for Him, new citizens with hearts that may one day be given to Him. God is an expansionist, not a protectionist. He wants to grow His kingdom, not hunker down and defend its borders. We are guilty of Too Many Players on the Field whenever we behave in ways that retard the birth and growth of whole, healthy families.

But the other way we violate the biblical injunction against Too Many Players on the Field is when we bring in "support troops" to seal a victory against our opponent.

This is the wife who says things like, "I think your bowling buddies are knuckle draggers—and Susan at the office agrees with me." This is the husband who says, "Bob's wife cooks a meal for the family every evening. Why can't you be like that?"

I am not suggesting that every man's choice of bowling friends ought never to be questioned, or that every woman's choice to work outside the home is a good one. What I am saying is that changes in family policy ought to be made by members who live under that policy—not by outsiders.

Spance ought to govern Spance.

And Frain ought to govern Frain.

But let those from Madagexico keep their comments to themselves.

Am I making sense here?

The Resurrection of Rodney F. Ultra-Light

PILING ON

**Work is like a bottle of booze;
you empty it, and then it empties you.**

I have only one regret about life with my dad.

It's an odd one, since it differs from the typical remorse one feels over "unfinished business" with a parent. Dad and I had no unfinished business—no promise unkept, no puppy undelivered, no paddling I didn't deserve.

It's only a minor stretch to say our relationship came to a perfect end one day, tied neatly with a bow of eight-pound monofilament, on a fishing expedition I'll tell you about in a moment. Still, I have this one regret. And the only way to put it into words is to begin a generation before my father, with the grandfather I never knew.

The sum total of my knowledge concerning my grandfather is that his name was William *Edward* Cunningham, the father of William *Alfred* Cunningham, the father of me... William

Welborn Cunningham. I know one other thing, and that is that my grandfather used to pitch for the Milwaukee Braves, back before they moved to Atlanta, leaving their former fans to stagger through decades of Brewer ball.

But that's it—there's nothing more in my memory banks about professional athlete W. E. Cunningham. Somewhere along the way, you would think his name would have come up around the dinner table, or in a bedtime story.

"Dad, tell me one more time about Grandpa and the mighty Milwaukee Braves."

"Well, son, they used to call your grandpa 'Gloveless Bill' because he's the only man to ever play bare-handed in the big leagues."

"Wow. You mean he didn't use a glove?"

"Couldn't afford one. He grew up poor, you know. Didn't own a pair of shoes until he was twenty."

"No shoes?"

"That's right. They almost called him 'Shoeless' while he was in Triple A, but he bought his first cleats before the nickname had a chance to stick."

"Did he ever make any cool plays…like…bare-handed?"

"Sure, he did. He caught one off the bat of Handlebar Paige in 1915 that shattered his wedding ring, and broke four fingers on his right hand. He still made the play to first, but he was out for the rest of the season."

"I thought wedding rings were for the left hand."

"Not when you catch so many line drives that your left knuckles are too swollen to fit a curtain ring over them."

"Wow."

"You better believe 'wow.' The old man was something else."

"Is that a true story, Dad?"

"If it's not, it should be."

But Dad didn't tell me that story. Instead, I got *Curious George* and *Babar the Elephant*, but never Mighty Milwaukee. Who knows what heights I might have reached, riding on the shoulders of Gloveless Bill? A little heritage can go a long way during adolescence, even if it is a bald-faced lie.

None of that matters now; I grew up in spite of the omission. What I'm trying to say is I regret my two sons have been on this earth for eighteen years, and I've hardly breathed a word to them about their own dead grandpa, William *Alfred*. For that matter, I've been speechless about William *Alfred* on nearly every front. It's as if some unseen enemy has placed a curse on me, and I am doomed to be as silent about my father as he was about *his* father.

Well, the time has come to put that regret to rest.

My dad was a big man—probably could have gone a long way in the majors himself if W. E. hadn't kicked off prematurely, leaving my dad fatherless at fourteen, with a wacky, whiskey-drinking cattlewoman for a mom, and the parting words, "Billy-boy, I don't expect you'll amount to much. You never could throw the curve."

We have a picture of Grandma Char sitting on a horse, a cigar in one hand and a glass of something flammable in the other. Her breath was like a dragon's. I spent the night with her once when I was a child. After we had sat up in our beds for a good hour, nibbling on wieners and donuts and watching *The Lawrence Welk Show*, we fell asleep, and I promise I could smell her snoring.

Eventually, Grandma Char converted from atheism to Christian Scientistism, and wasn't nearly as fun or entertaining. My mom introduced her to Jesus before she died, so I'm relieved to know I'll see her again.

Dad learned to ride at seven. By the time he was in high school, he was breaking horses and making money doing it. Most nights ended when the sun went down, seeing as electricity hadn't yet been strung in rural San Joaquin valley.

Dad once discovered a six-foot rattlesnake in his bunkhouse bed, killed it with a broom, and went to sleep next to its cold remains because he was too tired to fling it outside.

My dad was Paul Bunyan, materialized from the pages of folklore to father me. I could recount to you endless feats of double-decker tree houses slung together with nothing but wooden pegs; of road trips from Oklahoma to Colorado in the Country Squire station wagon, hand-painted by Dad himself; of a surgery he performed in our front yard one evening on a neighbor child who had gotten a #8 treble hook stuck through his eyelid.

Prior to my arrival on this planet, Dad had completed his ophthalmologic residency in southern California, where in his spare time he also learned to surf and oil paint.

There were only a few things my dad couldn't do, and nothing he wouldn't give to someone in need, except, if I'm honest...the gift of himself to me.

Now, I know I said there was no unfinished business between us. But what I meant to say was there was no unfinished business between us *eventually.* For the first nine-tenths of our life together, there was *very little* business at all. I got the dog, the vacations, the father figure cheering from somewhere in the crowd, and all the other amenities that come with being a doctor's kid, but I did not get the doctor himself. He was too busy giving sight to the blind.

Over time it occurred to me that no matter how much cheering my father did from the stands, there had always been a backstop between us. I might still feel the sting of that realization, were it not for the fated fishing trip I have promised to recount.

He came to catch rainbows with me one May, on the heels of a fight we had weathered during the spring of my senior year in college. It's hard to remember the details of our disagreement. Something about a "good father" being the kind who would have "bothered" to "take the time to hunt or fish now and then with his son." I recall words like *disappointment* and *failure* being cast at each other, along with the more incendiary, "You had your chance, old man, and you blew it."

I was twenty-one then. He was fifty-nine. I leave it to the reader to discern who said what. Nevertheless, there he was on my doorstep one May morning, decked out in a pair of red, overachieving chest waders that didn't stop until they reached his chin.

"Thanks for coming," I said.

"Wouldn't miss it for the world," he replied.

We drove in silence to the dock—Dad fidgeting with the various lures that hung from his ridiculous borrowed vest, fascinated by their appearance but blind to their function, and me praying I wouldn't say anything stupid like I did back in the spring. I paid for the rental boat myself, which gave me a strange rush of respectability, and soon we were chugging across the surface of dark Taneycomo.

Now, I don't recollect just how the conversation turned to W. E., but it happened all of a sudden, like the bursting of a dam, right as I was reeling in my fifth trout with my favorite ultra-light, "Rodney."

"I never could please him," Dad said unexpectedly.

"Who?" I said, giving Rodney a slight, upward jerk, and noting with thinly veiled enthusiasm that this fish was much heftier than the last. I also noted that my dad had caught nothing, which surprisingly didn't make me feel good at all.

"It was all about the curveball. Everything was about the curveball."

"What are you talking about?" I asked, trying to act more like a man who was patching up a relationship than one who was reeling in the largest fish of his life and had no real interest in talking. "Hand me the net," I added, glancing at Dad.

The faraway look in his eyes told me he was too preoccupied to notice our boat was being pulled sideways by the monster on the other end of my line.

"He never bothered to throw the ball with me."

"How about that net?"

"How could he criticize the way I threw?"

"Uh...I'm gonna need that net."

Like a trembling servant at the feet of its master, Rodney bowed almost to the water, and at any moment I expected him to snap. "Dad...please get the net now," I said more forcefully.

But he rambled on, lost in the 1930s. "All I really wanted was for him to take me to a game. Was that too much to ask?"

Suddenly the lake exploded into a billion droplets of light, and I saw the thing for the first time, dancing backward like Flipper across the water.

"Get the dang net!"

With the speed of a developing glacier, Dad flew into action. "The net, the net, where is the net? Son, what does the net look like?"

"You're sitting on it!"

"I am?"

Dad stood up and glanced at his seat, but there was no net to be found. All the while, Flipper was trying to dislocate my arm from its socket.

"Not on top of the seat! *Under* the seat!"

I reached over with my foot and tried to lift the seat, so Dad could see the compartment I was talking about. As I did, Flipper gave one last, mighty tug, and Rodney flew out of my hands, over the side of the boat and into the depths of Taneycomo.

Unintelligible sounds gurgled up from my own black depths, as I sat there watching both trophy and tackle disappear into their watery graves.

"We lost him," whispered Dad.

"*We* did not lose him," I snapped.

A hush descended on our boat, magnifying every sound, transforming it into an invitation for awkwardness. I closed my tackle box, and the snap of the metal clasp echoed angrily.

"I'm sorry."

"What are you sorry about?"

"I'm sorry about your fish."

"Who cares about a dumb fish?"

I jammed the key in the ignition and started the motor.

"Then I'm sorry I'm not a better fisherman, and I'm sorry… I'm sorry about Rodney."

I sighed and looked at Dad. Something about the way he was sitting there in the back of the boat, like an unemployed Orvis mannequin, made me wonder for the first time if maybe the reason he hadn't fished or hunted with me during my childhood was because his baseball-slinging father hadn't showed him how, and he didn't want to fail.

I gritted my teeth, still wanting to blame someone, but the image of a poorly thrown curveball kept sailing in and out of my consciousness, followed by the words, "Billy-boy, I don't expect you'll amount to much."

"You're a fine fisherman," I said, picking up a different rod and handing it to him. "Go on, Dad. Make a few more casts."

Much can happen in a moment, for both good and evil. Civilizations fall. Children are conceived. A streetlamp blinks on and lights the way for a tired traveler. The drowning of Rodney was much more than a personal loss; it was a pregnant moment, the culmination of all I had hoped for in a quarter century—the gaining of a father who was also my friend.

I cut the motor, and we drifted with the current. The fog had kept its appointment with the day, showing up at dusk as it always does on Taneycomo, cutting one's vision to nothing. Fifteen years in the future, I would have my own two sons on a similar fishing trip, and I would holler at the youngest for slamming another one of my rods in the door of our minivan. But for the moment, the future was blessedly obscured to me, and I could only see ten feet ahead to the nearest dock.

"Cast over there in that boat slip, and see who's home this time of day," I told Dad.

He gave his rod a flip, and sent his rooster tail up into the stall. WHAM! The water erupted like a geyser.

We operated like clockwork. Dad stood up, almost dancing with delight. I lifted his seat cushion, thrust my hand into the compartment, and retrieved the net, all the while shouting instructions.

"Set your drag!"

"What's a drag?"

"Never mind. Just be careful. Don't horse it! Don't horse it!"

With eyes closed and lips mouthing what I guessed was a prayer, Dad reeled frantically until his fish finally came into view.

"I'll be darned," I whispered. "Look what the fine fisherman has caught."

"What is it?" asked Dad.

"It's Rodney, back from the watery grave."

I let out a whoop and Dad opened his eyes. Together we leaned over the edge of the boat and stared at the gasping body of poor, dear Flipper, with two lures jutting from his hooked, lower jaw, and my beloved Rodney dangling several feet below him in the water. Back-to-back battles had worn the fish out so completely, there was no longer a need for the net. I started to scoop him up with my hands.

"Let him go," blurted Dad.

I slumped back against the seat, like a man who had been clubbed with his own left leg.

"Do what?"

"Let him go," he repeated sternly.

"Dad, this is the kind of fish men dream of catching. You and I just caught him twice. That means we should mount him."

"It means you should cut those lines, save your rod, and let him swim away, young man."

"Why?" I said, staging one last defiant stand.

Dad paused and looked at the fish. "Because somewhere down there on the bottom of this cold lake, he has kids he's dying to go home and see."

"You've got to be kidding. Fish do not have feelings."

"How do you know?"

I changed tactics. "Dad, this fish has lived a long time. Let's give him a nice home on your library wall."

"Nope," said Dad. "He has only just started to live. Cut him loose, son. His home is down there."

With that, I grabbed the line connected to Rodney, clipped off everything else at the lures' eyelets, and watched the largest rainbow trout I've ever seen melt into the shadows, two lures hanging from his crooked grin.

To my surprise, when I asked Dad if he wanted to fish any

longer, he was game for more. We fished until dark that day, but only caught a couple of trout for our efforts.

On my desk, I have a picture of Dad holding up two scrawny fish on a stringer and smiling as if one were Orca and the other Moby. Those were the first and last fish he ever landed this side of heaven. He announced his cancer to the family on Christmas morning, and by May he was buried in an Oklahoma wheat field.

Most boys grow up being introduced to others by their fathers. My own father loved introducing me—at church events, Rotary Club meetings, holiday dinners with scarcely known relatives. "Mr. So-And-So, I'd like you to meet my namesake and only son, Will. Son, don't you think you'd like to shake hands with Mr. So-And-So?" I heard it so many times, I could have saved everyone valuable time and simply walked around with my hand perpendicular to my waist.

But a curious fact of life is that most sons rarely return the favor until their dads are almost too old to shake hands with anyone. The closest I ever came to introducing my father was at his funeral, when I heaped word upon word of praise in his eulogy, as if I had been saving them for a special occasion.

I would give anything for a little more time with Dad—not just so we could fish, or hunt, or pal around at the gym together, but so I could introduce him to anyone who would listen.

God is the world's greatest dad. Even today, He still shows up to fish with His children, to catch rainbows, to create fishers of men, to chat into the wee hours of the morning. But mostly He comes so we might know Him more fully and make Him known to others. This is what it means to give God glory; it is to raise the world's opinion of its Maker by the way we live and talk.

Men and women who fall in love with God are unable to contain their affection. Inevitably they find themselves introducing Him to everyone in sight—friends, relatives, total strangers, in the same way I've introduced William Alfred Cunningham in this chapter. "Here is my dad, in whom I am well pleased!"

For some of us, it has been a long time since we introduced a doomed soul to our heavenly Father. Perhaps we are embarrassed of Him, or angry over some perceived abuse or neglect. Maybe we don't know Him very well and, therefore, feel an introduction of Him to others would be insincere...or worse, fraudulent.

Whenever we fail to do so, we leave conspicuous gaps between our faith and its object. Our silence is a trumpet blast, heralding something terribly wrong in the family of God.

Although it happened late in our lives together, my fishing trip with Dad opened the door to communication and friendship. Tragically, some kids never have a shot at such a relationship because their busy parents refuse to reform. I wonder if such kids purposely pick fights with their parents because negative attention is better than none at all. The results are devastating to Christendom; nothing lowers the world's opinion of God faster than when they see Christian family members sniping at each other.

If you want to rob God of His glory, here's a sure way to do it: Take your Day-Timer, or your Palm Pilot, or whatever you use to keep yourself on track, and fill it so full of "things to do" that you don't have a moment for your loved ones.

No time to wet a line. No time to throw a ball. No time to bake cookies, or go for a walk, or grab a milkshake at the DQ.

This will ensure that the next time you and one of your loved ones get crosswise of each other, you'll be primed to act like a grade A chucklehead.

Why? Because tired people fight with tired tactics.

In the early days of football, players were injured due to the absence of a rule—"piling on." Even after the referee blew the whistle, nothing prohibited a whole squad of players from diving onto a running back and mashing him like a pebble into the ground. It soon became apparent that without a rule, there would be no running backs left in the league. Thus, Piling On was born.

We all understand what it feels like to be under the pile. We live in an age of stress, where we "live to work" rather than "work for a living." All work and no play make Jack a dull boy. It also makes him a lousy fighter.

Excessive work, however, is not the only cause of stress. Other common stressors are weddings, newborns, deaths in the family, jobs that are lost, degrees that are always just about to be finished. Stress is the chief cause of messy fights. Every time I increase my pile, I increase my stress. Unfortunately, I also decrease my energy needed for healthy family fighting.

If you are constantly under the pile, and your relationships are suffering because of it, then you must first admit you have a problem on your hands. Like the muscle-bound lineman with a head of steam, your problem will not be halted easily. Remember, the greater the mass, the harder it is to slow it down. You are on a fast train to Coronary, which is a lovely town right next to Strokeville. You must do something about your stress. And in the immortal words of Jesus to Judas, "What you must do, do quickly."

Do you really want to win a family fight?

Then quit Piling On.

Quit adding to your to-do list.

Quit saying no to all those things you wish you had time for, and start saying yes to one or two of those holdovers from childhood that have never quite left you.

One of my goals in life is to live in such a way that I have stories to tell eight-year-olds. No eight-year-old wants to hear a story about what I did at the office today. He wants a story about fun, and a storyteller who knows his subject well.

This is what my wife wants, too. Cindy wants me to be fun, lighthearted, with some pep in my step at the end of the day. It's my own darn fault if I come dragging in the back door all pooped out. And it's doubly my fault if we get into a nasty fight.

Even as I type these lines, I have one eye on the clock and one eye on my computer screen. In just forty-five more seconds, I am going to quit typing, collect my things, check the mail in my cubby downstairs, jump in my car, and head home to throw the football with my sons.

I want to enjoy life. I want to eat cookies and thumb my nose at cholesterol. I want to catch Flipper before I'm too old. It's more important for me to love my family than to finish writing this book. I don't care if I'm midsentence. When that clock says it's 5:30, I'm

God

THE BUSINESSMAN'S BIBLE

The last thing my dad said to me before he died was, "We ought to fish more often."

Jesus was no stranger to stress. In fact, the stress He faced was hardly different from that of the modern businessman or woman. There was corporate opposition from the Pharisees, and the headaches of managing His disciples. There were the expectations of the masses that placed Jesus in great demand and called for an emphasis on public relations. And like today's executive, Jesus' job often forced Him to travel many miles and work late into the night.

Moreover, His family also contributed to His stress. He had to cope with constant sibling rivalry with brothers who saw Him as a man, but refused to worship Him as Messiah. There was the probable death of His father Joseph, when Jesus was a teenager.

Yet, in spite of these common stressors, we sense as we read about His life that Jesus knew the secret of mastering stress. *He let today's troubles be enough for today, and He didn't worry about tomorrow.*

No one has ever been quite as "present-minded" as Jesus. Who else could sleep peacefully in the middle of a squall at sea? Who else could calmly wash others' feet one evening, knowing His own would be pierced by nails the following day?

Thoughts

Jesus is the master of "the now." He alone holds the key to a stress-free life. And He alone can help you start taking things off your pile. Then you will notice a difference in your family fights.

But first you must walk with Him.

Slowly.

Deliberately.

And daily.

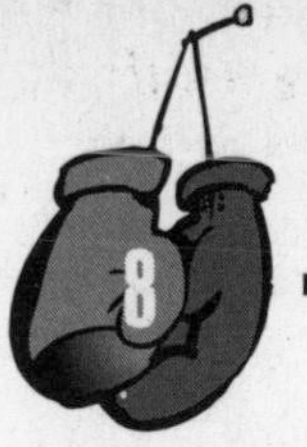

Rejected

GOAL TENDING

Goal Tending is what happens when one player blocks another player's shot after the ball has reached its pinnacle and is traveling down toward the cylinder.
I have never done it before,
because I jump like a water buffalo.

Before I tell you any more goofy stories about myself, or my kids, or my marriage, or my dog, or my neighbor's dog, or my past dating life, or my temper tantrums, or my gastro-miraculous recoveries, it would probably be a good idea for me to spend some time restoring the harmony between appropriate vulnerability and basic competence.

This will allow you to relax and know once again that you are not in the hands of a doofus. So, for the next few moments I am going to do some bragging. Here are all the great things I have done in my life, compressed into a space the size of a small tombstone. When I am dead and gone, please make sure the list gets put on the stone, so that people can walk by me and say, "My, my, my."

That would make me happy.

1. I was born in California. This automatically makes me cooler than everyone—except Mel Gibson; he could be born in Toledo and still be cool.
2. I moved to Oklahoma when I was three, and I have never, ever, ever been hit by a tornado. This is because of my cat-like reflexes. Plus, I am lucky—like a leprechaun.
3. I won the Phillips 66 "Pitch, Hit, and Throw" contest when I was eleven. Actually, I only won the local stage in Oklahoma City. When we traveled to Tulsa for the regionals I bombed out, and my dad bought me a hot dog, and we came home. He was a great dad.
4. I've played guitar since I was ten.
5. I also play piano, drums, harmonica, and dulcimer. Someday I am going to start a band and call it "Me."
6. I once provided some strumming while B. J. Thomas sang his famous song, "Raindrops Keep Fallin' on My Head." He didn't pay me a red cent.
7. I can do a backflip off of anything, no matter how high—as long as the water is deep enough, the wind is dead enough, and the lake patrol is absent enough.
8. I have eight screws in my hip, a half-pound of fishing line in my shoulder, no feeling in my left side, and on my worst day I still think I can lick all three of my sisters—one at a time.
9. I graduated from seminary *without* knowing Greek or Hebrew.
10. I have written four books. (Seven if we're counting this one, the one that got rejected, and the one that acts as a doorstop in my office.)
11. I have ridden a bull in Kansas, a camel in Israel, and a moped in Rome.
12. I have been a marriage counselor.

13. I have been a youth pastor.
14. I have cleaned pools and built fences and rolled pennies to make ends meet.
15. I sat on a rock once in Minnesota, and asked Jesus to come into my heart.
16. I told my best friend about Jesus—and he bought it.

    And finally…

17. I married a woman who doesn't need me…which means she probably loves me. At least that's what she said in front of the minister, and I believed her. Plus, it couldn't have been for my money. I didn't have any.

That's pretty much it. I don't want my stone to be too gaudy.

I remember being told in seminary that the two basic drives of all people are safety and significance.

The professor who said it was one of my favorites, and also a hopeless hyperbole addict. When he lectured, everything gushed from his mouth with the same mighty emphasis—like the Nile through a Pixie Straw. This made for a hoot of a class, but one's notes were useless. Everything was highlighted—*everything;* and underlined, too. It was impossible to tell what the man held dear. Occasionally, however, he would tip his hand, and the student who knew what to look for was the lucky stiff who got the *A*.

I remember the day he said the thing about safety and significance; he was sailing along, buoyed up by the flood of his own vast knowledge, when all of a sudden he raised up on his toes and a little bundle of bubbles was born at the corner of his mouth, like foam in a river eddy.

Immediately I highlighted the words *safety* and *significance*, then underlined them twice and scribbled a line of ocean waves above them, on top of which I added a stick figure of my professor hanging ten on the most important thing he ever said. And apparently it was *really* important, because I got an *A* on the next test—which is one more thing you can add to my tombstone.

I told you I was lucky.

Everybody wants safety and significance. We want to know that all is well and that we matter to someone.

This is a truth that people usually rush right past when they are fighting—like a runaway truck on a mountain pass, speeding by the exit ramp. "Yeah, I know I oughta pull this rig over, but I'm only doing ninety."

It is man's pitiful nature to look out for his own well-being at the expense of the other fellow's. I'll preserve my own safety and significance, and to heck with yours. If we were talking in basketball terms, we would call this "goal tending."

Wilt Chamberlain did a lot for the game of basketball. Other big men came before him, but no one was quite as dominant as the man from Kansas University.

Once he scored a hundred points in one game, and I'm pretty sure that after that was when all the other players got together at the bar and said we have to do something about this Chamberlain guy, or it's the end of the fun for the rest of us. So they widened the lane—which was a brilliant move; and nobody has come close to a hundred points in a game since then.

A hundred points, can you imagine? That's the kind of stuff

I dream about when I'm not worried about the underwear thing. Usually in these dreams I'm with a bunch of my friends at a gym, and we're involved in a pickup game where we're behind by, like, thirty points. All of a sudden, I go Doctor J on everyone. My hang time is unlimited. My shots are individual highlight films. I do crazy things as I'm going up for ordinary layups—wrap the ball twice around my defender's waist, bounce it off his forehead, sign it with a Sharpie, then make him dunk it *for* me. My friends can't believe how good I've become. After the game they grill me for information.

"Dude! Why'd you wait until you were forty-six to break out the skills?"

"Yeah, man—it must have been a bummer, sitting on the bench, knowing you could make Michael Jordan look like a rummy."

"I don't want to talk about it," I tell them, as I pump some air into my shoes and casually sink half-court shots.

If plagiarism is the mother of creativity, then embellishment is its nursemaid; and your dreams grow grander every time you tell them.

Note: Dreams are the only place you can wear shoes with pumps in them and still be cool. If you are not dreaming you should never wear pumps. Okay? So, let's review—no dreams, no pumps.

Everyone has a dream, because everyone wants to be somebody. Pain happens in family fights when we overlook this—when we act like our dream is the grandest one, and everyone else's is gutter trash.

Do you want to know the real reason they widened the lane in Chamberlain's day?

It was because ten men were meant to play the game of basketball...not one.

As long as Wilt could hang out in a lane that was narrow, nobody's shot was free from getting swatted.

Marriages and families are a lot like this, too. They are games intended for multiple players, not just one all-powerful, overpowering player. Everyone's shot is important—and needed. Goal Tending, or blocking one another's ideas, instills bitterness, creates distance, halts progress...and loses ball games.

My wife is five foot two; I am six foot four. She weighs about a hundred pounds; I am over twice that. She cannot remember her ACT score; I scored a twenty-eight on mine. She struggles to recall Bible verses; I have memorized whole books.

By all appearances, I am the Wilt Chamberlain of our household.

And yet...

Cindy is brilliant in an argument; I act like a baby and leave. She bakes coffee cake for the neighbors for absolutely no reason; I sneak hunks of it before it has been delivered. She can find Christmas gifts for forty-seven relatives on a crowded afternoon at the mall; I can't even find the dental floss in the medicine cabinet with a halogen lamp strapped to my forehead. She is the Proverbs 31 woman on steroids; I am Judas Iscariot on crack.

Cindy Cunningham is awesome!

Why in the world, then, would I ever *not* consider her goals of safety and significance as utterly important—even in the middle of a fight?

I'll tell you why if you promise not to laugh.

The reason I disregard Cindy's goals during an argument is because *I forget.*

It's true.

I genuinely forget how important it is for Cindy to believe that all is going to be well, and that she really does matter to me, to the boys, and to this world.

Here is how my forgetful process works.

"Don't you think you'd rather wear the red tie than the yellow one?" Cindy asks innocently, as we are getting dressed for church.

"No," I reply like a troll, bristling at the implication that I selected my tie this morning with nothing but mush in my head for thoughts.

Already I have forgotten Cindy's simple goal of significance—to feel good about herself because her husband looks handsome. Somehow in my pride and forgetfulness, I have misdiagnosed her benevolent desire for me to look my best as a malevolent design to control my world.

With my trollish reply, I have blocked her shot and am guilty of goal tending.

The ironic thing about goal tending is that the basket counts anyway, and he who committed the penalty ends up looking like a rookie. I can't tell you how many times I've still worn the red tie after acting like a troll.

If any of this causes you to recognize a flaw in your own approach to conflict, then try one simple thing: *Start validating everything your loved ones say.* This is the equivalent of my playing Cindy in a game of one-on-one and letting her take uncontested shots at the basket. Every unblocked shot is a validated shot. And the proper conversation about my tie might go something like this:

"Don't you think you'd rather wear the red tie than the yellow one?"

"That may be a good idea, honey. Why don't we hold it up to several of my shirts and see which one matches the best."

Now if you knew me, you'd also know that this conversation would never happen in my house, because I could wear Bermuda shorts and a Hawaiian shirt and be happy. But work with me, here; the concept is still one of validation.

And notice how I said *"may be"* in my response to Cindy—"that *may* be a good idea."

This doesn't mean I'm agreeing with her yet; it simply means that if Cindy is right, I benefit...and if I am right, she has gained the peace that comes from being validated.

Here are some other validating responses you can record on your cell phone and listen to over and over until you get them right:

- ★ "Sounds okay to me, let's explore it."
- ★ "Thanks for the input. I love the way you think outside the box."
- ★ "That's a fresh idea I hadn't thought of. I'm glad we're on the same team."
- ★ "It may not be the way I would have done it—but hey, who knows, it may work better than my way."

There are endless ways to tell people their goals and ideas are important, and yet it takes hard work to develop the habit.

Goal tending, on the other hand, is so easy it's sinful. Anyone can say or imply, "That's a dumb idea," and the results are as sad as Wilt Chamberlain's demise.

In the late nineties, Wilt Chamberlain boasted in an interview about his lifelong sexual escapades—their numbers so shocking as to be astronomical.

Later he died, and when they placed him in his seven-foot-long box and closed the lid I'm pretty sure he was by himself. The great rejecter of shots was now the greatly rejected. The man with the hundred points was now the man…

With nothing.

Validate, and your home will be merry.
Goal tend, and you will die alone.

God Thoughts

MAKING THE MOST OF OUR BAD DECISIONS

I love credit card commercials, particularly their recent ploy to pit civilized businessmen against the unwashed masses.

They want me to believe that if I have their card in my wallet I'll sail undisturbed through the fray, but if I don't, I run the risk of being attacked by mace-wielding Mongols in the middle of Starbucks. I think they think I'm an idiot.

And maybe I am—after all, I keep borrowing their money, and paying them back at interest.

Last spring, when I was traveling with some friends on a "guys' trip" (which mostly means we didn't have to stop for bladder breaks and raspberry tea every half hour), I received a phone call from my wife.

"Honey?" she said.

"What's the matter?" I replied automatically.

"Have you made any, um, unusual purchases with our credit card lately?"

"I bought some gas today. What do you mean by *unusual?*"

"You know—like two hundred dollars' worth of pizza in Gary, Indiana."

"Two hundred dollars—"

"Hold on, dear, that's not all. How about nine hundred dollars' worth of computer cartridges?"

"Nine hundred dollars!"

"There's more."

It was silent for a moment. Then, "Will?"

"Yes?"

“Don’t lie to me about this.”

“What—”

“Did you buy Final Four tickets for you and the guys?”

“No!”

“Where are you right now?”

“Oklahoma.”

“Okay, then, I believe you.”

“You believe me because I’m in Oklahoma?”

“No—I believe you because nothing as big as the Final Four ever happens in Oklahoma.”

“You’ve got a point. So tell me what’s going on with this…”

We talked long into the night, planning our next move, beginning with canceling the cards, making phone calls to the three largest credit agencies, and placing fraud alerts on all our new accounts. I even telephoned the FBI and talked with an agent about the situation. Soon we were hot on the trail of our perpetrator and learning more about his operation daily.

A phone call from a woman in Dayton, Ohio, enlightened us further. “I had been divorced for fourteen years, and was feeling kind of lonely,” said Tammy in a sweet Southern accent. “So I figured it was maybe time to get back into the dating scene. But I never should have gone online.”

That’s where she met Beckman—in an online chat room. Actually, she first saw a picture of him through a computer dating service, and she responded to his ad.

It seems the way our perpetrator worked was to find a

"needy woman" in an Internet chat room and begin wooing her. Beckman promised Tammy the moon. He said he was eager for her to join him in a business venture, one that involved shipping computer cartridges to his address in Nigeria. Tammy bought the sales pitch.

Soon she had nine hundred dollars' worth of computer cartridges in her basement—all purchased with my credit card. Beckman told Tammy that he and I were close friends and business partners. He would also be sending her a "Q" check for twelve thousand dollars, which she was to deposit in her bank account, keeping three thousand for herself, using a portion to ship the cartridges to his address, and mailing the remaining balance to him.

"If you want to see Beckman, go on yahoopersonals.com and click on 'Looking for Reel Luv,'" Tammy told me.

I followed her suggestion and was soon scrolling through a smorgasbord of Romeos. Eventually I found Beckman. He stood out like a Banana Republic salesman at a monster truck rally.

★ ★ ★

Here is some free advice to any guy who has ever searched for a date using one of these services, and come up empty-handed. Send a photo of yourself *without* a mullet or a partially exposed beer belly, and you will probably get some action.

★ ★ ★

Beckman had my social security number, my checking and savings account numbers, my credit card numbers, and even my signature—which he had mastered perfectly.

Tammy wasn't his only "girlfriend" either; he had seven others just like her scattered around the globe, each duped by his charm. All he had to do was sit at home in his Nigerian apartment, make online purchases in my name and wait for his ship to come in.

For the next few months, every time Cindy and I visited a restaurant or a service station, our credit was denied.

"I'm sorry, sir, but there seems to be some sort of problem with this card. Do you have other means of payment?"

It was a nightmare, but not one without a happy ending. After fifty thousand dollars' worth of fraudulent charges and a lot of help from the good people at MasterCard, Cindy and I finally believe we are in the clear. But you can never truly be sure when it comes to identity theft—the fastest growing felony in the world.

Goal tending in family fights is like never being able to get free of Beckman.

Your wife wants to try a new church, and you reject the idea without discussion. Your daughter wants to wear a belly ring, and you immediately think she's going to run away and join the carnival.

Thoughts

We all think we'd make pretty fair candidates to run the universe, don't we? It's a wonder any of us ever allows someone else to make a decision. Often the slightest proposal from someone sends us into veto mode, and we begin to goal tend.

But God does not goal tend. For our sakes, He lets us decide. Here is how God dealt with His defiant children, and how He committed Himself to not violating the rule of goal tending. Maybe you and I can learn a lesson.

"We want a king, and we won't take no for an answer!" badgered bratty Israel. "We want a real king…one we can see…just like all the other countries have!"

God knew it was not to Israel's advantage to have a king. Kings had a knack for starting armies, which inevitably led to the draft. Mothers would lose their sons to war, or at best to the drudgery of forging weapons. Others would be forced, without pay, to harvest the royal crops. The daughters of Israel would become maids of the court. And the king would seize their best fields and vineyards and give them to his friends. Being ruled by a king was certainly not in Israel's favor. Nevertheless, God granted their wish. And soon all of the above came to pass.

Saul enlisted an army of 330,000 men who had no choice in the matter. It was either fight for the king or be cleft in two.

David was a man after God's own heart. But he also had a heart for women, and his lust brought great tragedy upon Israel.

Solomon brought wealth and power to Israel. But like his father, women easily influenced him. And he took for himself

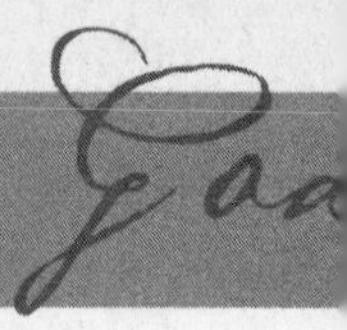

many foreign wives who led the nation into idolatry.

King Rehoboam's reign saw widespread homosexuality.

Abijah's stint was rift with civil war.

Self-appointed Zimri lasted seven days before he died on a pyre, having torched the palace to escape assassination.

Ahab and his First Lady, Jezebel, brought idol worship to new heights.

And Manasseh, whose name is synonymous with evil, practiced black magic and fortunetelling. He even sacrificed his own son on a heathen altar.

Finally, the moral decadence of the Israelite leaders rendered the nation physically and spiritually impotent. For five centuries, God had honored their wishes, allowing Israel king after king. Now they were at the end of the trail. And they found it led them back to where they had begun—as captives in a faraway land.

Sometimes God waits a long time to make good on our mistakes. It was nearly four hundred years before He allowed another king on the scene. Then one starry night, God proclaimed a new king. A special coronation was held in Bethlehem. The palace was a stable, the throne a manger. And the infant ruler was in stark contrast with his predecessors.

This king was pure and gentle, humble and holy. This king was peace loving, not warlike; wise, not foolish. This king is Jesus—the antithesis of that millennium between Saul and

Himself. And though many Jews still do not recognize Him, He is the king for whom Israel was longing.

What would have happened if God had said no to this king business and sent Israel to bed without any supper? Could they have avoided centuries of idolatry? Perhaps. Might they have missed out on Babylonian bondage? It's possible.

But what does the typical eighth-grader do when his parent says, "No go"? He heads straight for the nearest puddle of trouble and dives in. He does exactly what his parent told him not to do, and with an extra pinch of rebelliousness.

We can't be sure, but Israel probably would have done the same. Nevertheless, God gave them the freedom to decide, even though their decision was a bad one.

Are members of your family free to decide? Are their ideas and opinions accepted openly? Or do they feel as if Beckman has moved into your home permanently, and every time they try to use their MasterCard it gets rejected? If you answer yes to the latter, I encourage you to take a lesson from God: Learn to make the best of each other's bad decisions.

Obviously, discretion is necessary. Sometimes a parent must say no for the sake of the son or daughter's well-being. But as the child grows, he or she should be encouraged to take more and more responsibility for decisions. And by all means, do not major in the minors—don't prioritize rules over your relationship with your children. This only provokes them to anger and bitterness.

God Thoughts

Teens whose parents enforce values as well as the freedom to decide usually do not stray from those values. They may rebel, but unlike children who have been harnessed to household rules, they don't resent their parents.

Finally, a spouse should never treat a spouse as a child. You are joined together in marriage to help one another *reach* your goals…not swat them away. The marriage that is characterized by a consistent rejection of each other's ideas begins to resemble my relationship with stores and shops after Beckman worked his evil magic. Too many family fights include negative statements like these:

"That's the most hideous hairdo I've ever seen. You head right back to the salon and have it fixed."

"Dear, you're too old to start your own business. Besides, you're not trained for it."

Maybe the hairdo and the business venture *are* bad decisions—so was Israel's election of a king. And hair grows; the business might fly. It took many crummy kings in order for God's children to learn a lesson. But God gave them the freedom to experience the worst.

Then He gave them Christ, the picture of a true king. And in doing so, He made the best of their bad decisions.

Asleep in the Eternal City

TRAVELING

If I could take the entire city of Rome and squeeze it into my stomach...there would still be room for one more gelato.

With all this talk of *"winning"* a family fight, *"enjoying"* a family fight, everything turning up "*roses*" in a family fight, surely some reader out there has gotten his hackles up.

"Fighting can't be all this fun," I can hear some of you saying. If this describes your thoughts, why not turn immediately to the back page, write down all the contemptuous things you'd like to say about the author, and then, whenever you're ready, simply hurl this book in the trash can and say, *"Chercamo una tavolo alle esterno!"* (which in Italian means "I'm looking for a table outside"...or something along those lines).

This may seem irrelevant to you, just as it did to most of the people I sprung it on in Rome a few years back. But like I've always said, when you find a foreign phrase that pleases your ear, insert it in as many conversations as possible.

Need a taxi? *"Chercamo una tavolo alle esterno!"* Want a single dip of chocolate gelato? *"Chercamo una tavolo alle esterno!"* Real Italians will think you're a moron. But your friends who know even less Italian than you will be stunned right out of their Caravaggios...which are either an expensive pair of sandals from Florence, or a famous painter commissioned by one of the popes. I can't remember.

How strange it is to admit that on my one trip to the cradle of Western civilization, where I was surrounded by such wonders as the Sistine Chapel, the Forum, and the Coliseum, my favorite memory of Rome was riding motor scooters in the maniacal Roman traffic.

Let's all pause now and say the word *maniacal.* It is a good word, because it fits the loose order that passes as "traffic laws" in the Eternal City—which, by the way, probably earned that nickname because its drivers are eternally homicidal. I still have the claw marks on my stomach where Cindy sunk her nails to keep from flying off into a melon vendor's cart.

If you want to experience the safest way to get around town in Rome, put a blindfold over your eyes and walk down the middle of the street. They tell me the penalty for hitting a pedestrian is the loss of one's license *for life.*

Herein lies the clearest illustration of the Italians' adoration of the human body, despite a detached regard for everything else material. Tony Minestrone, careening his tuna-fish-can-of-a-car down the cobbled streets, will do everything in his power to avoid striking Aunt Tia and her sack of Turano bread, but will not think twice about sideswiping a bus, or leaving a legacy of auto paint on a sixteenth-century statue.

★ ★ ★

It is my firm belief that the Roman Empire never fell; it simply lost its driving privileges.

Rome's tastes and smells are so lively, you pray for an extra mouth and nose. Row upon row of glistening gelato greets you around every corner, making it impossible to choose a flavor without scheduling an afternoon.

"I'll have mango, please."

"Bella," says the shopkeeper.

"Oops. Sorry. I think I want pistachio. Yeah, that's what I want."

"Mohte bella."

"Umm…can I switch to cappuccino? I can? Great. Wait a minute. Put it back."

"*Perdon*?"

"Put it back! Put it back! I want chocolate! I gotta have chocolate! *Chercamo una tavolo alle esterno*!"

"Are you an idiot, signore?" says the shopkeeper, shifting to perfect English.

"No sir, I'm a tourist. I come from a land where they offer thirty-one flavors of gutter trash and call it a treat. Would you please, please, please put one scoop of each glorious flavor into that wooden barrel over there, and let me wallow in it for an hour?"

"Quit scaring the other tourists."

"Gimme gelato!!!"

"Here's a free scoop and five euros for you to leave my shop before I call the polizia."

What I'm struggling to say here is that gelato doesn't rival American ice cream; it buries it. When I arrived in Italy I was content with Baskin-Robbins, and when I returned home I was a gelato slave boy.

Help me.

Then, there are the flowers. Freshly cut bouquets decorate even the most dismal of alleyways, their vendors dozing in the intoxicating sun, as if to say, "Go ahead, steal one. Everything else in this town is stolen."

I was surprised to learn how many of Rome's masterpieces used to belong to someone else, usually the Greeks. Poor, pitiful Greeks. It must be hard to live a hop, skip, and a jump across the sea from the neighbor who ripped you off. But at least the Greeks weren't alone. Eventually, Rome took the whole known world to the cleaners. Everywhere you look, there are signs of their thievery.

Obelisks? Stolen from Egypt.

Temple menorah? Stolen from Israel.

Marble? Stolen from everyone.

Sistine Chapel ceiling? Not stolen; but Michelangelo was virtually forced by the pope to get the job done, when all he really wanted to do was chisel away at his dream piece, a house-sized chunk of marble that never did get completed. So in a sense, Rome even found a way to steal a man's time.

Time. Now there's a relative term. We Americans are mighty proud of being just a tick over two hundred years old. But to the Romans, the powerful descendants of the once peaceful Etruscan farmers, our country is an historic hiccup. In the time it has taken us to grow up, the Romans had already sacked a continent, seated a couple hundred popes, rescued Christianity from the clutches of evil emperors, watched their own religious household be ransacked and then reupholstered as the two vastly different abodes of Protestantism and Catholicism, developed blueprints for machines that could fly above the clouds and swim on the ocean floor, and created the world's greatest place to ride a scooter.

Time is nothing to a Roman.

Then again, time has left its mark on Rome. One glance will tell you that Boredom, the spoiled offspring of Time, has run amok in the Eternal City. Graffiti is the national art form, and there is no shortage of artists.

I saw "Go home, Bush!" on the side of a bus, and wondered which news agency had shaped the artist's opinion. It was decent artwork, technically, but inspired little in me except homesickness for Missouri.

Boredom is a wicked little boy, barbiturate in nature and disastrous to the home that harbors him. He cast a spell over Rome long years ago, and it appears nothing can wake the city from its slumber. How else does one explain Rome's Gothic ghost towns, also known as "cathedrals"? You will find one every few thousand meters or so. Beautiful...tragic...empty.

Oh, how the cradle of Christianity has become a divan for the drowsy. Great men of Rome, too familiar with the Divine and bored out of their skulls with His blessings, began to call themselves gods, and wound up feeling contemptuous toward the one true God.

Two thousand years after the reign of the Caesars, this same boredom is evident in their offspring. One sees it everywhere in Rome, in the eyes of leather craftsmen, wristwatch hawkers, plaza vendors, and cafe waiters, whose dull expressions suggest they have sold the same bruschetta to the same tourists day after day after day. To their credit, they are friendly enough, and perhaps the handsomest race I've ever seen. But just let the topic veer toward Christ and they are suddenly mute, unable to converse about the figure that hangs on countless crosses around their lovely town.

Rome is *us* a few centuries from now, asleep in her own squalor. Everywhere you look, pornography leers at you from billboards. Dogs relieve themselves at the base of masterpieces. Homeless people sit in the center of busy thoroughfares, their Styrofoam cups held upward for the odd coin. And right down the center of it all walks the most gorgeous Italian couple you have ever seen, leather-clad and lean, fresh off the runway, their noses as high as the Great Dome at the Vatican. They do not notice the homeless person, or the fact their beautiful city is coming apart at the seams—or the shrill horn of the scooter, speeding toward them like a bullet from a gun.

Sometimes I think I am the "walking man" James Taylor was singing about—I walk to get from A to B, but I also walk just to feel alive. We walked everywhere in Rome, Cindy and I—that is, when we weren't courting death on motor scooters. We walked to the Spanish steps, and all the way to the top of them. We walked to the Coliseum, and saw where the Christians were killed for their "walk." We walked to the Forum. We walked to the Vatican. We walked in search of gelato, and pastries, and pizza margherita, and that romantic feeling people promised would overwhelm us when we finally found the Trevi Fountain. We walked, and walked, and walked.

Traveling brings out all the seldom-used emotions in me; it dusts them off and sets them in their proper places.

Traveling has also been my undoing.

★ ★ ★

People say I walk just like my dad, and I tend to believe them. I can feel it sometimes, when I'm not really thinking about it. I feel his arms swinging like they were my arms, his right hip dipping, his feet moving slowly to their own music. It is banjo music—rolling up and down the neck. People are never in a hurry when they listen to banjo music. They may clap their hands and stomp around a bit, but nobody's going anywhere. Not far, at least.

Maybe it was the banjo music I was concentrating on all those times I used to travel when I played basketball. Yeah, that must have been it.

"Tweet!" went the referee's whistle. "You're traveling, number seventeen."

"It's the banjo music," I would say. "It has my feet going faster than my hands. I can't get it out of my head."

"Gimme the ball, banjo boy. Next time, keep dribbling while you're moving."

I think the people who make the rules for basketball should come up with a better name for traveling—maybe "loitering." Traveling sounds too, I don't know, productive or desirable. I find myself wanting to do it simply because of the name.

I like the fact this chapter has a rambling feel to it. It rambles from Rome, to the basketball court, to the back porch of some old, toothless banjo picker named Lester.

Some traveling is like Lester's rocking chair: It gives the traveler something to do but doesn't really get him anywhere. This is the kind of traveling that people do when they walk out on a loved one in the middle of a fight. They get their feelings hurt, or get tongue-tied, or get afraid that some irreparable damage is about to happen, and all of a sudden they're gone. Just like that. They might be in Rome visiting the pope, or eating a wheelbarrow full of chocolate gelato, or maybe filing for divorce. This is the problem with some traveling…nobody knows where the traveler has gone.

I wonder what the church would be like today if the first Christians had run away from hard times.

"Excuse me, sir? Mr. Centurion?"

"What do you want?"

"Is that a lion you're about to unleash in this arena with me?"

"Yeah—what of it?"

"Uh, I think I'd like to become a pagan—where does one sign up for the pagan thing?"

Once, when I was on vacation with my family in Disneyworld, I got mad at Wesley in a restaurant and went to the van and drove off. This was very strange behavior, seeing as I left a whole steak and my family sitting back at the table, wondering where I was going. *I* didn't even know where I was going. To ride some roller coasters? Maybe catch the fireworks display by myself at the Magic Castle? I drove about a block and came back to the restaurant. Everyone was still sitting there, and everything was exactly as I had left it—except it looked like someone had taken a bite out of my steak.

This is the funny thing about traveling. After the traveler has gotten it out of his system, he still has to come home and face the people he left. It seems like it would save a lot of gasoline and shoe leather if he just learned to talk.

But what do I know?

I'm just the walking man.

And the walking man just walks.

ANYWHERE BUT HERE

Sometimes I tease my wife about our first date, about how I wrecked her car and got her naked. But she always wants to argue the details.

"You did not *get* me naked, Will Cunningham."

"You looked naked to me."

"They *cut* our clothes off at the scene of the accident. It's not as if I *threw* myself at you. I was *unconscious*, for crying out loud."

"Well, I'm not trying to insinuate that you remember anything…or *saw* anything."

"I don't…I mean I *didn't*. I didn't *see* or *remember* a thing."

"Of course you didn't."

"That's what I've been trying to tell you."

"You're absolutely right, C—you've been telling me that for years."

"Then we should drop the subject."

"It's okay by me."

"Fine."

"Okay."

(Pause)

"Of course…I remember EVERYTHING."

"Stop it, Will—just stop it."

"I'm pretty sure the paramedics remember, too."

"Will!"

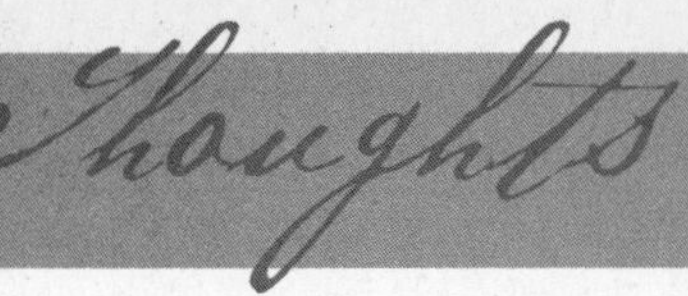

★ ★ ★

When I woke up in the hospital after our car wreck, I was happy—for about two minutes. Then as the morphine cloud burned off, I gradually became aware that something was not right with the left side of my body. The realization began with my fingers. I remember dragging the tips of them along the bed and wondering why the hospital had given me sheets made of broken glass. I pushed the little button by the side of my bed, and the nurse answered. "Bring me some normal sheets, please," I said. And she told me that normal sheets were the only kind the hospital used. So I hung up and looked at my fingers—but they looked just fine.

Next, I recall a breeze blowing on my left cheek. It was not a pleasant breeze; it was more of a hot breeze—like a demon from hell's barbershop was giving me a shave with a blowtorch. I found the source, a nearby electric fan, and pulled the plug.

What's wrong with me? I wondered.

There were the obvious things. My face was a country road of stitches, which my fingers explored ever so lightly. A metal pin disappeared into my knee on one side and emerged again on the other. It was attached to a sort of hammock, which in turn was fastened to three or four cables that were connected to a pulley that was somehow loosely affiliated with the frame of my bed. By the looks of things, I had extended reservations in this hotel.

But what was wrong with the *rest* of me?

I studied my right hand—wiggled my fingers, dragged them across the sheets, felt my face.

Nothing.

Everything was normal on the right side of my body.

But on the left side—it was all blowtorch and broken glass.

And it wouldn't go away.

I have often wondered what it felt like to Jesus when they drove the spikes through His hands. I mean, right when the sharp tip plowed through the skin, and the capillaries, and the carpals—did it send a jolt to His brain? I can hardly stand a splinter in my finger; He must have had a thousand of them embedded in the goo that was once His back.

Before I understood the way the Trinity worked (which, by the way, I still don't fully), I imagined that somewhere in the middle of the crucifixion Jesus entertained the thought of getting even. I envisioned Him with one powerful surge ripping His hands and feet from the points where they were impaled, grabbing centurions by their tracheas and tossing them around like sheaves of wheat.

But then I went to seminary, and the sharp people there told me I had an overactive imagination and that my thoughts on Jesus getting even weren't actually biblical. They told me that God the Son had a role to play in the Trinity, and that He played it to the hilt. He was not an angry victim, bent on revenge; He was a suffering servant, willing to hang in there and suffer for everyone—even the crummy old centurions.

I think about these things a lot, and I wonder why I can't hang in there when a simple family fight gets a little tough for me. It's not like anyone in the family is trying to crucify me.

And it's a good thing, too—because I'd make a lousy Savior of the world. The first time that whip fell across my back, I'd come undone.

"Hey, I don't need this! Do you know who I am? I'm the Lord of the Universe. I could be anywhere but here right now if I wanted. In fact, I'm out of here. Somebody hand me my robe. You with the whip—what's your name? I've got my eye on you."

"It's a brain contusion," said the doctor, when we finally got the chance to chat about the blowtorch and the glass.

"So how long is it going to last?" I asked. "A week? Two weeks? Maybe a month?"

The doctor didn't try to soften the news—good doctors never do.

"Well, son, it's just like the eight screws in your hip—you'll probably have it for the rest of your life," he said. And then he walked out of the room, proving why doctors would make great centurions.

That was the first time I recall feeling sorry for myself in the hospital. I lay there sour and depleted, like a half sack of lemons, thinking of all the things that had been instantly changed for me because of the car wreck.

I won't be able to jam on the guitar anymore.

I won't be able to jog.

I won't be able to play basketball, or tennis, or anything else that requires legs.

And to top it all off, my face looks like Freddy Krueger.

Me.
Me.
Me.
Me.
Me.
Me.
Me.
I was pathetic.

An old song from my childhood says, "It wasn't the nails that held Jesus to the cross"—and I agree. I think what held Him there was the knowledge that if He didn't go through with it, *I* would have to someday. Maybe at the very moment those spikes were screaming through His hands, Jesus could see me in His mind's eye, far out in the future, paying for my sins, struggling on a cross in front of a righteous Judge. And He knew that I couldn't even stand a splinter. So He stayed up there.

I like that about Jesus. If anyone had the right to "travel," it was He.

But He never did.

Twenty-five years after the accident, I've gotten used to having feeling only in my right side. It's perfect for boxing with my boys; I just lead with the left side of my face and I never feel a punch. And guitar? That's been a little more difficult to overcome. It took a long time to retrain myself, without being able to feel the strings. But when I keep my eyes on my fingers, they usually do what they're supposed to do.

Life as a half-man has been a whole lot better than I thought it would be, back when I was feeling sorry for myself. Cindy has been great about it. When we go for walks around our neighborhood, she always positions herself on my right side so I can feel her hand. Sometimes, just for variety, we switch places and everything feels awkward. Once I looked down at our hands while we were walking in the moonlight, and I noticed my numb hand in her scarred one—the one she thought I would never find attractive again; my wounds pressed tightly against her wounds.

Never believe someone who tells you two wounded people can't be good for each other.

We are all a little wounded.

That's not true—we are all *mortally* wounded, with great, gaping holes in our carcasses that only the Savior can mend. I wonder why, then, we make things worse by walking out on one another when our conflicts get heated. Do we suppose wholeness lies somewhere out there, away from the loved ones with whom we are fighting? Do we imagine we'll somehow benefit from "traveling"?

Take it from a half-man. We are never more whole than when we hang in there on behalf of those we love.

Holy Bowling

PICK UP THE SPARE

Picking up the 7–10 split is like saving a baby from a burning building: People imagine you were planning it all along.

It wasn't my fault Eddie showed up at the house that night with a "let's-go-siphon-some-gas" look in his eye.

I do not want to be judged for the company I kept in the tenth grade. Nor am I half the fool I was in those days. But there was something about Eddie, something so attractive that if he had been a flame, and I a moth, nothing would be left of me today except a pile of bug-ash and high-tops.

It was mid-fall and I was cutting our grass at the buttery end of a Sunday when I heard Eddie's car coming up the block. I tried like mad to hide, honestly, but when he saw the handle of my mower sticking out of my dad's holly bushes, Eddie called me out.

"The night's young, Cunningham. Me and the boys are going bowling, and you're coming with us."

"Can't do it, Eddie," I said, crawling out of the bushes on my hands and knees. "I got chores still, and my sister's birthday is tonight."

Besides being a bald-faced lie about the birthday, this was also a weightless appeal to family loyalty, seeing as Eddie didn't give a rat's rear end about his own family.

Eddie grinned. "You chicken?" he said.

"What—to go bowling? Yeah, right, Eddie—I'm real chicken. *No,* I'm not chicken. I'm just tired of bowling. That's all."

"This isn't your ordinary bowling, Cunningham; this is *special* bowling," said Eddie. He revved the engine, and I heard laughter coming from the backseat of his Trans Am.

"Hey, Rich. Hey, Vince," I said, waving to them like a third-grader. Vince and I had fought once in grade school, and even though he always insisted on telling people he won the fight, I never recalled it that way.

"You coming or not, dork-face?" said Vince.

Now, I have many flaws, but I have never been a dork-face. With my resolve reduced to nothing, I slunk into the house and begged my parents to release me from our Sunday evening routine of popcorn, soup, and *Lassie.* A minute later, and with the family blessing secured, I roared away with Eddie into the unknown.

I should have guessed something was wrong when I saw the six bowling balls on Eddie's floorboard; when we blew past the Highlander, the scales fell from my eyes.

"You missed the bowling alley," I said, struggling to achieve an incidental tone.

"We've already been there tonight," said Eddie.

I glanced at the balls again, and the words *special bowling* took on special meaning. We rode around until it was dark, plastered to our seats by the sounds of Jethro Tull and Bad Company on the eight-track. After an eternity, we pulled into a shadowy neighborhood.

"Here's a good one," said Eddie, slowing to a crawl.

"Perfect," said Vince.

Rich just sat there, giggling. He never said much of anything, which in a funny way was the reason I trusted him the least.

We were on a lonely thoroughfare, darkened by the absence of streetlights and yard lamps. It was past suppertime by then, so most homes had only the blue glow of TV coming through their curtains.

"Roll down the windows," ordered Eddie.

We responded like automatons, and immediately the car was filled with the chill of October. I have always liked October, in the same way a kid likes horror movies and ghost stories. Something about the way it smells—like a gray sky weeping. It's hard to explain, but my nose understands. To the east I saw the moon rising like a silver sickle over the rooftops.

"What's this got to do with bowling?" I asked.

"Don't worry about it, Cunningham," whispered Eddie. I knew right then he had heard the trembling quality in my voice.

Darkness swallowed everything except for a desolate, white rectangle at the far end of the pavement, which, when I finally got my bearings, informed me the street we were on was perpendicular to another street. And where the two streets formed a *T,* there was a driveway and a house.

"What do you think, boys?" asked Eddie.

"It's like a runway," said Vince.

"Yes, indeed, it is. Almost like it was made for us. So, who's feeling lucky tonight? Who has a good frame in him?"

Vince and Rich each picked up a ball and scooted to opposite sides of the back seat. “Oh, I got a good frame in me,” said Vince. “You better believe I got a good frame.”

Rich giggled and hung his left arm out the window.

“I'll punch the chump who throws a gutter ball,” said Eddie as he pushed the gas pedal to the floor. “Here we go!”

Now, to those who have never been in a car that was built before the gas crisis, before the air bag, before the catalytic converter and the concern for the ozone, you have only known what it's like to travel quickly. But you have never known how it feels to be strapped inside a death-defying-date-crying-nearly-flying-hunk-of-U-S-of-A-steel-on-wheels, with a decal of a phoenix the size of a Quik Trip gas station and a ridiculous scoop in the center of the hood, the purpose of which is known to nobody. This was the American muscle car, and it was measured in horses—not liters.

It was awesome.

It was also like pulling G's in the space shuttle.

When we reached a hundred and fifteen miles per hour—I promise I am not making any of this up—I suggested to Eddie that it might be a good idea to slow down before we blew a tire, or hit a parked car, or went into orbit and became a satellite. When he didn't answer, I began to suspect he was okay with any of these possibilities, and I began to scream like a schoolgirl.

“Eddie, you slow this car down right now, or I will not ride with you ever again!”

The only response was a smirk, and a yammering chorus of howls from Rich and Vince.

“Eddie!”

“Ed!”

“Edward!”

Frantically, I searched for the magic word his mother must have used to call her little monster to the table, and the only one that would bring these 440 horses to a manageable gallop. Rich giggled and leaned dangerously out of his window. Vince did the same. Sandwiched between the two of them, I felt as if I had been taken hostage by a terrorist bowling team.

"Make it count!" shouted Eddie. "And no gutter balls!"

Faster and faster we went. A hundred and twenty. A hundred and thirty. A hundred and thirty-five. With each second that ticked by, the house in the distance drew closer.

"When I hit the brakes, you let 'em fly!"

Suddenly, the physics of the thing that was about to happen dawned on me, and I opened my mouth with one last appeal to reason.

"You don't seriously mean you're going to roll a bowling ball through that house—do you?"

Eddie smiled, as if the idea intrigued him. "We've never actually had one go through a house," he replied. Then he began to count, and all I could do was close my eyes at the horror movie that was unfolding in front of me. When he reached "three" there was a terrible screech and I opened my eyes in time to see two black projectiles streaking away in the headlights, and disappearing with a thunderous *BOOM!*—straight through the garage door.

"Did you see it?" squealed Eddie as he wheeled around the corner and sped toward asylum. "Did you see how easy those balls went through that stupid door? It was like it was made of butter! That's what it was—butter!"

It seemed more like insanity to me.

I never went "bowling" again with Eddie, but I often wondered what would happen if a family was out taking a walk one evening when those three decided to show up. Two months later, in the dead of January, Eddie called me to brag about their escapades.

"Pick up the newspaper," he cackled. "I think you'll get a buzz from the society section."

I went downstairs to see if my dad was finished with the paper and found it lying in his favorite chair. I opened the paper to "Talk of the Town" on page seven, and this is what I saw:

VANDALS STRIKE AGAIN

Under the headline was a photo of a gentleman posing for the camera on his driveway with two bowling balls, and behind him the mark of my idiot friends. Scanning the article I discovered that the victim's house was the same one we had visited on that terrible night so many weeks before. And when I looked closer at the picture, I saw that there were not two of Eddie's holes—but four.

He had come back for the spare.

Please do not e-mail me with complaints about my choice of stories. I am not flaunting my past; if anything, I'm trying to redeem it. I'll use anything to illustrate the devastation of family fighting, particularly if it shocks a reader into change. I hope by now you recognize I use tales of sports and leisure to make a point.

And here is the main point all over again, newly minted and polished for your benefit:

Every family fight is like a sporting event. There are two opponents. Both want to win. And most of your fights happen on the weekend.

Eddie's vandalism was a "gutter ball" compared to the "strikes" that happen in so many family fights around the globe. I am not being cute, here. In my counseling office, I have watched family members roll through each other like a sixteen-pound ball through a tenpin. At times the tears were so abundant, we abandoned the tissues and used our sleeves. I have seen a CEO behave like a wolf, ripping his wife's esteem with his words, and then feeding on her raw, exposed soul. I have seen a Christian housewife admit her sexual affairs, just to see her husband whimper like a child. Usually when the ball gets rolling with this much inertia, it's impossible to stop the carnage; but occasionally I have witnessed a family recover before things got out of hand.

This is what I call "picking up the spare," and it is an indispensable part of a good fighting strategy. Just as there are secrets to beginning and ending a good family fight, there are also secrets to salvaging a poor fight—even right in the middle of one.

When I was first developing the concepts of *Family Fight,* I sensed it was important to tell people how they could begin and end a fight properly. But more than anything, I knew I had to provide hope for those of us who sometimes find ourselves knee-deep in the middle of a poor fight, and nothing we try seems to be working for us.

Bowling provided the answer. And in a strange way, even my memories of Eddie's vandalism found their way into the equation. Eddie was tenacious, like an unwelcome dog in the neighborhood, or a bad cold, or Ted Kennedy. No matter how often you thought you had seen the last of him, he always displayed his staying power, and he wouldn't quit until he finished what he started. The point is that the person who doesn't quit in a fight is like the bowler who stares down a 7–10 split and winds up getting the spare.

Cindy and I were in a fight once, way back in the Dark Ages of our marriage. I was ridiculously busy with seminary, learning how to study the Bible with hermeneutics, how to capture the "big idea" of a text systematically, how to diagnose people with the help of the *Diagnostic and Statistical Manual of Mental Disorders*. Hermeneutically speaking, I was becoming a very no-fun person to be around. And it didn't help matters that Cindy was on the Pill.

Right in the middle of our fight, at that point when you begin to wonder if the people in the apartment on the *other side* of the apartment next to yours have turned their TV off and are listening to you instead of Ted Koppel, Cindy said something that has changed our fights forever.

"You are *not* my enemy," she said.

"Yes I am!" I insisted. I tried not to smile, but the more I surrounded myself with the sandbags of opposition, the more ridiculous I became.

Cindy's smile came freely now. "So you want to be my enemy?"

"Yes!"

"Even though I don't want you to be?"

"All the more so!"

"Hm. It doesn't sound like you're going to have much of a battle if I walk over there and kiss you on the lips and tell you I love you and then walk away."

I was smiling now, too; I couldn't help it. But it made me so mad, because I wasn't through fighting yet. I scrambled to regain the higher ground.

"Don't you dare do that, you...you devil-woman. I've heard about women like you. It says somewhere in the Bible that I should flee from women like you."

"I think you're referring to a harlot."

"Then that's what you are!" I shrieked. "You're a devil-woman harlot who is trying to harlotize and demonize the time-tested and decent practice of fighting that every decent..."

"I'm coming over there to kiss you right now," said Cindy.

We both started to laugh uncontrollably—the kind of laugh where your pants could be covered with fire ants, and you'd still be yukking it up as they chewed off your kneecaps.

"Get away from me, devil-harlot!" I said, scurrying around to the other side of the breakfast table.

"Kiss! Kiss! Kiss! Kiss!" cried Cindy, giving chase. She was wearing slippers, and I was in my socks, so she had the advantage on our wood floors. I think we ran around like that for five or ten minutes, until one of us took a detour down the hallway to our bedroom, and then I can't be sure, but I'm pretty sure that exactly nine months later Peter Fowler Cunningham was born into our family.

And that's how you pick up the spare.

Seriously.

I'm not kidding.

If, for instance, you happen to get into a fight with your spouse—say, this evening after you have read a chapter or two of this book—and things start to get out of hand, you don't have to sweat it anymore. Why? Because you know the secret of Picking Up the Spare. You know how to turn a bad fight into a good fight simply by changing the way you think about your opponent.

Your spouse is not your enemy.

Your kid is not your enemy.

Your boss is not your enemy.

Your neighbor is not your enemy.

Eddie, and Rich, and Vince are not your enemy.

The only one who is your enemy is that miserable snake who has sworn himself to enmity with God until the end of time. It's high time you started taking shots at him instead of your loved ones.

I don't care if your wife has slept her way through the neighborhood, or your husband has a mouth like a paper shredder. Even if divorce seems to be your only option, you are never free in God's eyes to treat a human being like an enemy. We are to love our enemies. And the second we begin to do that, our enemies become objects of love. They are lovely, lovable, beloved—nothing like the monsters we imagined them to be.

I am a terrible bowler. The older I get, the more terrible I become. I am mostly terrible because I'm *inconsistent.* One day I might bowl a 200, and the next day a 48. It also doesn't help that I'm six foot four and look like Ichabod Crane on a night out with the guys.

I wish the bowling alley employees would see me coming, and just automatically put those inflatable bumper pads in the gutters. Then pretty soon, old Ichabod Crane would be up at the snack counter, laughing, and playing loose with his money, and buying nachos for everyone.

Sometimes, I wish I had those bumper pads for my marriage. That way I could take whatever ridiculous kind of shot I wanted at Cindy, and she would still think I was awesome.

> "I'm home, honey—and boy, am I starved! What's for dinner, woman?"
>
> "Darling, I don't feel very well. I think I'm coming down with something, and I may need to lie down for a while. I can't be sure...but it feels like avian flu."
>
> "Mmm. That's just awful, dear; I had my heart set on Chicken Marsala. Oh, well...you can always grill some burgers. I'll give the chicken to Scout."
>
> "Thanks, honey. I knew you'd solve it; you always know just what to say. You're also a hottie and very romantic."

But I know it doesn't happen like that at my house.

I am not a hottie, and my marriage does not have bumpers. If I take a lousy shot at my wife, leaving nothing but the 7–10 split, it's not up to anyone but me to make the most of my poor play. Nobody is going to pick up the spare for me. Sometimes when we're in the middle of a difficult conflict, we just have to take a deep breath, select our ball, and go for it. As I said before, it works wonders to say the phrase "You are not my enemy."

Then watch what happens.

You step up onto the wood. Your approach is smooth and effortless. You bend deep, and your follow-through is impeccable. As the ball leaves your hand, you don't even watch for the results. You simply turn around, pump your arm like Kirk Gibson, stroll back to the scorer's table, and mark a slash in the box.

That's the way you do it, friends.

That's the way you pick up the spare.

Every time.

HOME FOR THE HARLOT

As always, I want to convince you that the rules in this book are not made up by me—rather, they are ancient, biblical rules that have been around forever. I merely want to open a new window or two, through which you can *see* old truth. That makes me a carpenter of sorts, or a window-craftsman. Call me what you want.

If God were a bowler, then the story of Hosea would certainly be a 7–10 split. Fed up with Israel's whoring around with idols, a lesser god may have hit the Reset button and started the game over. But in Hosea, God makes a conscious choice to pick up the spare.

He calms His anger.

He disregards His sorrow.

And He selects for himself two unlikely new "balls," one a prophet and the other a prostitute, with which to do His work.

"Hosea," says God, "I want you to go and take to yourself an adulterous wife and children of unfaithfulness, because the land is guilty of the vilest adultery in departing from the Lord."

Hosea obeys. He marries a whore named Gomer, and they start having kids together. Now, it is wild enough that a holy God would instruct a holy man to hook up with an *unholy* woman. But when we see that God is going to use this marriage to teach a lesson to unfaithful Israel, and that Hosea and Gomer's children will also be used, we hunker down for a good read, because we know we're into a page-turner.

The first child born is named Jezreel after a valley of the

same name, and with him comes God's warning: "I will put an end to the kingdom of Israel, and I will break her bow in the Valley of Jezreel." God was tired of His people's half-hearted romance with Him, and he wanted them to know He was withdrawing His patience and protection.

The second child is named Lo-Ruhamah, which means "I will no longer show love to the house of Israel." God was brokenhearted because of Israel's infidelity, and He wanted them to know He was withdrawing His love.

The third child is named Lo-Ammi, which means "Not my people." God was angry at Israel's idolatry, and He wanted them to know He was withdrawing their privilege of bearing His name.

The cool thing about all this is that God chose a burned-out, used-up whore to get His message across. That had to count for something, don't you think? Surely, those who knew Hosea well made the connection. They must have seen right away that Hosea was the God-figure in the story—and that left Gomer as the character that represented the whole miserable pack of Israelites. Maybe they saw God's point. Maybe they saw that no matter how much whoring around they did as a nation, in the end God would always be their faithful husband.

I love this.

So much of the Old Testament seems like a bad game of bowling. You know the kind I'm talking about—you roll a three in the first frame, two gutter balls in the second frame, a two in the third and the fourth. By the time you get to the midway mark, you are pretty sure you couldn't hit the broadside of the universe if you shortened the lane by thirty feet and made the pins the size of Volkswagens. I've often wondered why God didn't just start over; there would have been no shame in that.

I think God keeps reaching out to His people because He knows we're all messed up. If it had been the Americans who were His chosen ones, or the Germans, or the Polynesians, each of these groups would have made the same boneheaded mistakes as the Israelites. Why? Because we're all boneheads, and boneheads act boneheadedly. I'm just thankful God chooses to pick up the spare instead of starting over.

Oh, how the Creator loves the things He creates. He loves His children, even when they turn out to be whores and whoremongers. Gomer was glad of that.

God loves Eddie, and Rich, and Vince, too. He offers them His love, His name, and His inheritance. This makes me think I, too, ought to love the Eddies of the world. And if I can do that, then I know I can love my wife, and my kids, and my friends and neighbors, no matter how dismal the game of conflict becomes for us.

I am going to pick up a lot more spares this coming year; I can feel it in my Ichabodish bones. When I get in fights with people, I am going to tell them quietly in my heart, "You are not my enemy."

I am not going to be discouraged when I look down the lane and see a 7–10 split. Instead, I will dry my hand off, select my ball, make my approach, and let it fly. Then the place will erupt with applause, and I will take off like a maniac, leaping from lane to lane, laughing, shouting, buying nachos for all the local harlots who have come tonight to pick themselves out a good man to settle down with. And finally, when every person in the bowling alley has abandoned his bowling, and everyone is dancing, and I am standing on top of a pool table, waving my shirt and doing some sort of mambo—then the bowling alley employees will tackle me, and put me in a straitjacket, and ask me what in the Sam Hill I was doing.

"I picked up the 7–10 split!" I'll explain.

And they will understand.

And all will be right with the world.

Until I arrive home, and Cindy asks me why I smell like a pack of Camels nibbling on cheese dip.

The Law of Golf

FIXING YOUR DIVOTS

I am Jed Clampett on a golf course.

Forgiveness is at the heart of golf and family fights. It is ancient, and everything swings upon it like a hinge. I've seen forgiveness in small ways and large—some that shouted for attention, and others that passed by unnoticed at the back of the parade. My friend Dale Ray is so far behind the parade he can't hear the noise of it, on account of the thick walls at Potomac Correctional Facility.

Now, I've been a friend to embezzlers, porn fiends, serial adulterers, and those who smoked pot for lunch. But Dale Ray is my only murderer friend. Visiting him at Potomac is nothing like visiting normal civilians. One has to get permission first, then drive two hundred miles to the middle of nowhere, then pass between rows of razor wire, then take off most of his clothes and be inspected for hatchets, knives, screwdrivers, and hairpins, then scurry through six or seven steel gates (all of which lock behind you with a deafening *thud*), then be interrogated by Sergeant Stoic, and when you finally arrive at Dale Ray's cell, you are deep in the bowels of Potomac Correctional Facility.

Seventeen years ago Dale Ray shot his drug dealer—blew him away with a shotgun over a pound of substance that can transport a man's mind to Shangri-la or lock him away in a box. He has been at Potomac ever since, locked away in the maximum security of Missouri's most infamous prison. Once they put him in solitary for twenty months straight, and he almost forgot the sound of his own voice.

So much has passed Dale Ray by since he entered Potomac—the warmth of sunlight, the scent of cinnamon, those parts of the parade us "outsiders" take for granted. He has also missed the invention of the Internet, the cell phone, karaoke, frozen custard, Bill Clinton, both Bushes, and seventeen Christmases with his family. By law, he does not deserve a single blessing or freedom.

And yet.

Dale Ray is the most blessed man I know, because he has embraced the law of golf that sets men free.

People who need forgiveness are the loneliest people in the world. People who need to *give* it are even lonelier.

I do not know how old the earth is, or whether science and religion should even bother trying to be friends. But I believe there was once a time when men called caves "home"—and it was not so long ago.

We have three great holdovers from cave days—fire, water, and golf.

First there is *fire.* Nothing in all the millenniums of discovery even sniffs the one that was made that day when Grock and Oggie were coming in from the hunt with rabbits slung over their shoulders. Suddenly, Oggie was smitten by a fulminating power from the sky, and Grock soon found out that roasted rabbit tasted better than raw. When he had left that morning on the hunt, Grock was a boy with a rumble in his belly; but when he returned to the clan that night, he was a sovereign lord with power in his hand—the power of light, heat, smelts, iron tools, iron blades, warfare, world travel, space travel, and hamburgers.

Nobody even asked what happened to Oggie.

The dictum for authority today is what it is because of fire. *He who possesses a smoldering branch is king—as long as he keeps it smoldering.*

Second, we have *water.* One has only to turn the faucet handle and he is reminded that all water comes from bygone epochs. Raindrops that fell outside Grock's cave are still falling today—merely recycled. Cave water was in Dale Ray's orange juice this morning at Potomac. It was in his shower, and in his mother's windshield wiper fluid as she drives the two hundred miles to visit him. At lunch, Dale Ray and his mother will meet in a little room adjacent to death row. They will eat sandwiches from the vending machine, washing them down with quiet sips of the water Jesus walked on.

Everywhere we go, we are awash in a river of antiquity.

And finally, there is *golf.* Golf is the tribal hunting party that disappeared with the dawn of agriculture, but then reemerged in a new, yet no less primitive form. Still raw and haunting for those who partake, golf requires little more than sticks and stones and a brave resolve to do battle in a meadow with something much bigger than men.

So, men still go to the meadow.

They leave behind the soft world of the foragers and the fire tenders, and they go out in numbers—foursomes usually, though not constrained to fours. They hunt for birds. They hunt for eagles. They bolster their courage with nicknames like Tiger, Golden Bear, Shark, and more. And sometimes they don't come back to their caves until long after sunset, and it is too dark to hunt. It they are lucky, they bring the spoils.

Golf is the missing link between the past and the present; and the law of golf is what binds each dispensation together. What is this law? It is forgiveness in its most tender form. No other sport draws all men together, regardless of their race or creed…or handicap.

Golf is primitive, but it is not for Neanderthals. Players must be gentlemen and noble ladies. Players must make right their wrongs. The law of golf demands they "fix their divots."

True golfers, the ones who care about the game in the same way cavemen cared about the hunt, are never in too big of a hurry to bend down, retrieve their divot tool from their pocket, and make amends to the ground they have damaged.

In a way, the golfer who fixes his divots is saying "I'm sorry" to the grass, to the Course Marshall, and to the players in the foursomes that follow.

"I am sorry, grass—I am sorry I have bruised you. All my good intentions have left you pocked and forlorn once again. Here, let me knead your tender blade; let me soothe, and smooth, and heal the wounds that I have caused. Please forgive me. I depend upon your health for my success."

The beauty about golf is this thing called a "mulligan." It's like a do-over. I use them all the time when I play.

Sometimes I wish I could have a mulligan as a dad; there are so many things I'd like to do over. But there is no such thing as a dad-mulligan. There is only the hope of forgiveness and forgiving.

In spite of all my mistakes, I think I have taught some very fine things to my boys—one of which is the importance of saying, "I'm sorry—please forgive me." Wes and Peter will forget most of the righteous things I have modeled in our home. The odd thing is, though, they will never forget the times I asked forgiveness for my unrighteousness.

This is divot fixing, my friends. It can be done in the lonely corner of a prison, or in the living room of your own home. But the important thing is that it is *done.* Fix your divots—fix them today. Don't advance to another hole until you have repaired the damage behind you.

I do not know whether Dale Ray is a golfer. I imagine he takes more of a liking to coon hunts and catfishing. But I know Dale Ray has been touched deeply by the law of golf. His divots are gone now—forgiven and healed by Jesus on the day he kneeled by his cot and spoke with Him. If he could, Dale Ray would make amends to the outsiders whose lives he harmed. He would say, "I'm sorry—please let me fix my divots."

But for now, Dale Ray is in Potomac for life, so he can't do much divot fixing. He used to be on death row, until the pope came to town about five years ago and chatted with the governor of Missouri about pardoning him—and the governor agreed, lifting Dale Ray's death sentence just a few hours before he was to be injected with a lethal dose of sodium pentothal.

It's funny how quickly things change. Both that governor and that pope are dead now, and Dale Ray is still up there in Potomac sipping holy water.

God Thoughts

KEEPER OF THE GREENS

From dust, God created man. And out of man, He fashioned woman. As their Keeper, His design was for them to flourish and to become lush and green, and He provided the perfect climate for them to do so. They were to God as the golf green is to the groundskeeper—precious and beautiful.

But something spoiled God's greens: sin. And in sorrow, He watched their color fade from bright emerald to pasty grey. Yet He did not abandon them. Even today, He kneels faithfully and fixes the divots with a tool called forgiveness. No divot is too big for Him to repair.

Rummage through the pages of the New Testament and you will uncover some pathetic men and women whose lives were pocked with divots. One in particular stands out in the eighth chapter of John's Gospel.

> Half naked and dirty, the woman was dragged to Jesus and thrown at His feet.
>
> "Take a look at her!" shouted her accusers, the religious leaders of Jerusalem. "We caught her red-handed. What should her punishment be?"
>
> Clearly the woman was at fault. She had committed one of the three gravest sins of her day—adultery, which, along with murder and idolatry, was punishable by stoning. The smug Pharisees stood with their arms folded, waiting for Jesus' answer. If He condemned her, He would be stripped of the title "Friend of sinners"

and would lose His following. If He set her free, they could accuse Him of teaching others to defy Jewish law. They had Him cornered—or so they thought.

Jesus surprised them all. He had compassion for the woman. He saw her in a manner unlike the Pharisees did. True, she was in conflict with God. She had willfully broken one of His commandments. By choice she had put a monumental divot in her life, severely damaging one of God's greens. Had the Pharisees not confronted her, she would probably have gone on sinning, leaving behind her a trail of unfixed divots. But Jesus envisioned her as she was meant to be—smooth, soft, and perfect. Instead of naked and ashamed, He saw her clothed and full of integrity. Rather than empty and searching, He saw her brimming with joy.

To the Pharisees He said, "Okay. Go right ahead and stone her. But let him whose life is void of divots cast the first stone."

Slowly, the crowd dispersed. Soon the woman was left standing alone with Jesus.

"Where are your accusers?" said Jesus. "Didn't even one of them condemn you?"

"No, sir," she said.

"Neither do I," said Jesus. "Go and sin no more."

The woman came to Jesus with a sin-pocked life, and walked away forgiven. She had met the Keeper of the Greens…and He had fixed her divots.

Thoughts

I have often wished that all of life could be flawless and tranquil, like a perfect golf green. The Pharisees wanted the same. They longed for a world where everything was in order and the rules were kept. But they were unwilling to deal with divots.

Take a divot inventory of your household. Start by checking your own list of dos and don'ts. Every family has one of these, whether it is written on paper or kept in the head. Here are a few entries from the list Cindy and I keep:

- ★ Thou shalt not make entries into the checkbook without subtracting.
- ★ Thou shalt not wear muddy shoes in the house.
- ★ Thou shalt not leave home with the curling iron turned on.
- ★ Thou shalt not gamble on a low gas tank.
- ★ Thou shalt not leave the toilet paper roll empty.

Maybe you recognize one or two of these. You can be sure that each time one of your commandments is broken, another divot is driven into your life. Often, the offender neglects repairing the damage. He or she wanders off without so much as a simple "I'm sorry." That's usually when the sparks begin to fly.

Successful family fights depend on forgiveness. That doesn't mean you have to abandon your sacred list and let others walk all over you. Jesus did not do that. To the woman caught in adultery, He said, "Go and sin no more." Nevertheless, He was tender and compassionate as He dealt with her.

God Thoughts

That is exactly how Jesus wants us to treat one another—with tenderness and compassion. He wants us to say "I'm sorry" when we put a divot in someone's life. And He wants us to say "I forgive you" when someone puts a divot in us.

"I'm sorry."

And "I forgive you."

If only golf could be this easy.

What Do "They" Know?

MATCH THE HATCH

They say 90 percent of the fishermen catch 10 percent of the fish.

They say a bad day of fishing is better than a good day at the office. But a recent fishing trip with a friend of mine shows that once again, "they" cannot be trusted. In fact, "they's" quote is only true when *both* fishermen are having equally bad days. The trip with my friend, whom we shall call "Doug" (since that's his name), defends this point.

Doug and I have fished together for fifteen years, in all sorts of weather, and on all sorts of water. He is my closest friend besides my wife.

Most of our excursions have proven Doug to be the better fisherman—an honor he attributes to the fact that he is a fly fisherman and I am a bait caster. Doug, you see, is a self-proclaimed fishing fascist who looks down his nose at anyone who does not tie his own flies, build his own rods, or consult the Cabela's catalog as if it were the Bible.

I, on the other hand, am the ultimate river redneck, unashamed to dangle a night crawler in the rankest of water, using filament so thick and old it doubles as a stringer. This explains why Doug usually catches more fish than I do.

On this particular morning, however, that statistic was meaningless.

In a stiff wind, and from the slender confines of our borrowed canoe, Doug whipped his masterfully tied bucktail streamer—until it got masterfully wrapped around a nearby sandbar willow.

Meanwhile, as Doug wrestled with that merit-badge-of-a-knot formerly known as his fly line, I chummed a half can of crickets into the water and proceeded to catch more fish than Jerry Rice used to catch footballs, commentating on each of them.

Needless to say (though I think there is a need), Doug did not congratulate me on a single catch. And after an hour of unpleasantness, during which Doug pointed out every flaw in God's plan for placing that particular willow in that particular spot, he finally severed his line with a knife and motioned for me to steer him to shore, so he could be alone in his depression. I can only assume this was his intention, because he had not spoken directly to me since somewhere between my cheerful announcement of the twelfth or thirteenth fish on my line.

Anyway, the point I am making in all of this is that when we approached the shore, and Doug began the delicate task of stepping from a tottering canoe onto solid ground, the inevitable happened.

This, by the way, kids, is the same reason it is never a good idea to jump out of your mom's minivan while it is moving…or leap off a merry-go-round that your older brother has worked up to light speed. It's a physics thing, but I was an English major, so don't ask me to explain it.

All I know is that when Doug placed one foot on dry land, the canoe began to push away from the shore, and Doug's legs assumed an angle that they (I am sure) will never reassume.

When the seat of his waders was a scant trout's-nose away from the water, things got really funny.

Now, of course when I say "funny," I don't mean funny in the collective sense, as in Doug thinking it was as funny as I. No, it was funny in the way a pie in the face is funny...or a businessman slipping on a banana peel is funny...or, say, a fly fisherman, dressed up like an Eddie Bauer model, falling into the water is funny.

It was very, very funny.

It was so funny that I laughed until Doug's soggy head bobbed back into view, and I saw that he did not share my good humor. Except for the dozen or so minnows that got sucked into Doug's hip boots when he took the plunge, we did not catch any more fish that day. And that was okay with me.

Why am I telling you this?

I have no idea.

Oh yes I do.

The reason is not to somehow suggest I'm a better fisherman than Doug. The fact is, if you took all the fish we've ever caught and stacked them up, Doug's stack would tower over mine like Goliath over David.

It's just that I happened to be there on the day he took a fall, and I want to point out that a similar kind of fall can happen to the best of us.

Love takes a plunge whenever we stop being students of our loved ones. Like the fisherman who thinks he has mastered everything there is to learn about fish, the person who thinks he knows his spouse so well he can afford to slack off is in for—

A plunge.

Now, I love making fun of Doug, but the real reason he catches more fish than me is because he has never stopped thinking like a fish. One particular thing Doug has taught me about fly-fishing is that the fisherman must always "match the hatch."

Matching the hatch is a time-consuming procedure. It involves finding out what the fish are eating that day and then matching it with an artificial morsel that looks similar.

Usually the smart fisherman will walk downstream, away from the "holding waters" where he intends to fish. Then, with the help of a screen, he will sift the surface of the water hoping to catch evidence of the "carte du jour." A bug, a fly, a tiny fresh-water shrimp…any of these might be on the menu that particular morning, and the wise angler doesn't want to be caught serving the wrong thing.

This all takes extra effort, of course, but once you've matched the hatch you are way ahead of the other fishermen on the river. While they're dangling all sorts of unappealing baubles in the water, you'll be ringing the dinner bell…and catching fish.

Let's review. For catching fish, you have to give them what they like. Just any old thing won't do. Start throwing in every fly or lure under the sun and they'll swim on by faster than you can say "Zebco."

The same thing applies to a family fight. If you plow recklessly into your opponent, you'll most likely scare him or her away from what could have been a successful confrontation. But if you take the right approach, you can woo your opponent toward resolution.

★ ★ ★

Fighting with your family is easy. Fighting *properly* is harder than catching a trophy fish. Why? Because fish worth catching are elusive.

Fighting properly with your family members requires you to Match the Hatch. In other words, you must never, ever, ever stop thinking like one of them. This is difficult, I know, because so many of the thoughts I think are about *me*—and I'm worried that if I start thinking about Cindy, or Wes, or Peter, all the un-thunk thoughts about myself will swim away like fish that have snapped the line.

But this is nonsense.

To fight well with Cindy, I must think like Cindy. I know this sounds impossible, but this is coming from someone who, on the advice of Doug the Fishing Fascist, once crawled on his belly for twenty minutes through a high-country bog at six in the morning, with a Royal Coachman fly dangling from his #2 tippet, just so he could arrive undetected at the edge of Delaney Butte Lake and make the first cast of the morning—and all of this after cutting open a native cutthroat from a nearby inlet and inspecting its gut for the morning menu.

I caught a four-pound trout on that cast at Delaney Butte—please believe me when I tell you that Matching the Hatch works.

Over the years I have learned many things about Cindy that have helped me be more successful in fighting with her. I have learned that because she is five foot two, she feels more comfortable if I sit my six-foot-four-inch carcass down during a conflict.

I have learned that she is attracted to me when I buy her a laundry basket because the old one is broken, or when I fix the garbage disposal, or when I replace lightbulbs.

I know this sounds weird, but I have also learned that when I do these things they earn me special powers, like in a video game.

One power is the ability to be Selective Listening Guy. It allows me, in the middle of a fight, to miss part of what she is trying to tell me, and then when she discovers that I have been thinking about, say, fishing with Doug instead of her, she acts as if I am cute as a bug, and the fight goes much better.

And all of this because of a 75-watt lightbulb.

(Other powers include Drink Out of the Milk Carton Guy, Hog the Remote Guy, and Late for Dinner Guy. However, Jump in the Van and Drive Away Guy does not work at our house. When I try to use that special power, Cindy turns into Drop Off Your Own Dry Cleaning Girl.)

These are just a few of the things I have learned that fall under the category of Matching the Hatch.

Do you know what size your wife's feet are?

How about her dress size?

Do you know that when she offers you advice, it might not be because she wants to control you—but because she loves you?

Do you know her tones of voice?

Do you know the tones you use that make her feel insecure or under attack?

Do you know her cycle? (Not like a Harley—the other kind.)

Do you know which things you do or say to the kids that make her think you hung the stars?

Can you name even one of your family traditions? Have you ever initiated it?

Do you know the way your wife prefers you to comb your hair? Do you care?

All of this may sound silly to you—particularly the men. But when did we get the notion that one lifetime is enough to get to know a person? When did we settle for the contempt that familiarity breeds? If I lived a hundred lifetimes with Cindy I would still know only a sliver of her soul. Familiarity only breeds contempt if I have ceased to look for that which is *un*familiar in Cindy.

To put it simply, I don't want to know my wife in this lifetime—I want to still be introducing myself to her when I die.

Fishermen who come roaring up to the riverbank in their Yukons, yakking, hollering, and slinging their shiny, nine-pound lures all over kingdom come will always be part of the 90 percent of fishermen who only catch 10 percent of the fish.

But those of us 10 percenters who sneak, and whisper, and crawl through the grass, and study the *Curtis Creek Manifesto*—well, we've got 90 percent of the fish just waiting for us to catch them.

In a quarter of a century, Cindy and I have never fished together. But I am not sad about this, because I know my wife well enough to know there are other ways she'd rather spend time together. So, we have "fished" in other ways.

We have flown kites in Denver.

We have sampled cakes in Jerusalem.

We have ridden scooters in Rome.

We have driven Ventura Highway in a convertible.

We have petted manta rays in the Caymans.

We have prayed on the rim of the Grand Canyon.

We have fought in Maui.

We have hunted crabs in Destin.

We have served in soup kitchens.

We have snarfed down deep-dish pizza in Chicago.

We have bought pottery in La Jolla.

We have made love by the fireside, in a tiny, insignificant cabin, deep in the woods of the Ozarks.

We have taken the time to know each other, to "match the hatch" if you will, and because of this we are hopelessly on each other's stringer for life.

BULL

HOW TO START A FIGHT

When I look at a lady's hand purse, it's hard to imagine it was once a bull.

I watched my Lab, Scout, open up shop on a stray this morning, and if I hadn't been writing this book on fighting, I would have done something to break it up.

Instead, I took notes. Here is how to start a fight if you are a schnauzer.

First of all, you should abandon your sense of timing. You are never going to establish yourself as the baddest dog on the block if you're always concerned about time and the other fellow. It was 6 a.m. when I stumbled outside to water the flowers, and I saw this little guy, this bandy little never-been-in-the-neighborhood-before Hitler of a pup come goose-stepping down the street like he had just bombed Great Britain. He sat down at the end of my driveway and commenced barking.

"Me! Me!"

"Me! Me! Me!"

"Me!"

"Me!"

"Me!"

I did not like Hitler, so I squirted him with the hose and he marched off to conquer my neighbor Robert's driveway. This time he did not announce his arrival. Instead, he went about saluting the trees, and the bushes, and the back tires on Robert's minivan, as if to say, "Here are the exact spots where the bombing will begin."

This is the second thing you must remember if you want to start a fight properly. You must never be overly conscious of your neighbor's rights, or his space, or anything that pertains to his own comfort. You are der Führer of everything you see. Go ahead; make your mark.

Now, Robert's dog is old, and feeble, and fat, and was lying next to the tire Hitler had just saluted. Checkers is a good-hearted creature, but honestly, he looks like a five-gallon water cooler with fur and legs. I think Robert feeds him lard, or Little Debbies, or something. But it's none of my business. Far be it from me to tell another man how to take care of his dog.

Anyway, from where I stood on my lawn, watering the lamppost distractedly, I could see that Checkers had his eye on Hitler. He did not want him in his yard, or on his driveway, or anywhere near his people. They were a peaceful community, Checkers and his clan—neutral, like Switzerland or Texas. If this fellow thought for one moment that he could march in there and start giving orders, then he had another thing coming to him.

The little dictator started barking again, this time to taunt his elder.

"Fat!"

"Fat!"

"Big, fat, fatty-fat!"

Checkers stood up and ambled toward Hitler. He looked like John Wayne in *The Cowboys*, where he has to fight Bruce Dern for the herd, and he gets the snot beat out of him, and ends up dying for, like, only the second time in all his movies. It was a really sad movie. I found myself standing there in my pajamas in my front yard at six in the morning, rooting out loud for a dog that reminded me of The Duke.

"You show him, Checkers. Don't let that fascist push you around. Let him know who's boss."

But Hitler rose to the challenge, charging before Checkers could even get his fat going in the right direction. For a moment the subdivision held its breath, and then there was an explosion of fur in the middle of the driveway.

The fight was on.

"Get him, Checkers!" I hollered.

When Scout heard me choosing sides, she cast her vote and took off running to defend her friend.

"Atta girl, Scout," I said. "Show ol' Hitler how we play around here."

Like the Americans at Normandy, Scout hit the driveway full speed and took a few cuts on the chin and chest before Hitler felt the brunt of her fury. With a yelp he scampered off into the woods, and nobody has seen or heard from him since.

I was so proud of Scout I gave her a pat on the head and a Pop-Tart for her courage.

Let's review. If you want to start a fight, and you are a schnauzer:

1. Forget about timing. There is no time like the present to be a jerk.
2. Think only of "me."
3. Disregard your opponent's space, feelings, rights, etc.
4. Use ugly slurs and overgeneralizations.
5. Attack swiftly.
6. And hope that your opponent doesn't have a big, hairy, loyal friend with fangs.

I am glad I'm not a dog. My temper is such that I think I would be dead by now if I were.

Actually, if I were a dog I'd probably be the kind of dog that had a lot of friends. They would laugh all the time at my jokes, and invite me to spend the night because I'm always good for a story or two. And then one day they would hear the news that I was down at the dump with my master, sniffing around for Little Debbies, and I went postal on a poodle for piddling on my master's shoe.

"Poor Billy," they would howl. "He was such a gentle cur. I wonder what caused him to snap?"

Billy would be my dog name.

It's good to be human, isn't it? They say we are the only ones amongst God's creatures who are able to exercise self-control. Sometimes this seems like hopeless theory to me, particularly after I've acted more like a dog than a man. But I like the sound of it, and I love the way it feels when I get it right.

★ ★ ★

Man alone has the knack for holding anger back.

I was just kidding about starting fights; I don't think that's such a good idea. Later on in the book we'll be exploring together what it means to *end* a fight, and how to do it; so I thought it would be important for us to at least consider the front end of a fight, too.

Dogs start fights.

People *stumble* into them.

I don't believe in starting *or* stumbling.

I believe in *preparing* for life—both the good and the bad.

Preparation for a fight is crucial.

Here is something that happened to me once that might make you buy the preparation thing. I mentioned John Wayne a minute ago, and that is probably because I admired him as a fighter. He once said, "A cow ain't nothing but a whole lot of trouble tied up in a leather bag." My first experience in a rodeo makes me think he would probably say the same thing about bulls.

It started with a phone call in 1992. I was writing books and building fences at the time, which means I was unemployed. Wes was five, Peter was three, and with Cindy as a full-time mom, the bills were piling up.

"Phone's for you," said Cindy, one warm spring evening. "It's Lyle. I think he has something up his sleeve." She was smiling as she handed me the telephone, but her eyes sent a message of their own: Don't do anything foolish. We don't need a paycheck *that* badly.

If it had been anyone but a world-champion cowboy calling, Cindy would have just handed me the phone and gone back to whatever she was doing. But this was Lyle Sankey, the bareback, saddle bronco, and bull-riding champion of the planet in the late 1970s. He wasn't just calling to chat. Lyle always had something up his sleeve.

"Hello?" I said suspiciously.

"Got plans for the weekend, city slicker?" asked Lyle. He hates formalities.

"I was just going to mow my lawn."

"Ya ain't raisin' grass, pardner—you're raisin' boys. The grass can wait. Why don't you pack some bags and bring your citified selves up to Abbeyville, Kansas, for my rodeo school."

"You mean, like, to watch?"

"Heck, no. I need a hired holy man for the weekend. I want you to talk about Jesus to my cowboys."

"But no animals, right? You're not going to make me get on any animals."

"Course not."

"Lyle?"

"Trust me, pardner."

Never trust someone who likes falling on his head.

Whatever demon possessed me to say yes to Lyle's request must have come straight from rodeo hell, because three days later I was packing my van and herding my family to Abbeyville.

"Yippee!" said Wesley, when I told him we were going to a rodeo.

"Yahoo!" added Peter.

"We're nuts," I muttered as we pulled out of the driveway. Cindy patted my hand, and off we went on the six-hour journey. When we arrived at the rodeo school, we might as well have landed on Pluto.

"Are you all right?" asked Cindy.

"There are a lot of hats and boots here," I replied.

"That's what cowboys wear."

"I have Chuck Taylors and a Chiefs cap."

"You'll be just fine."

But I was not just fine. I was the Marlboro Man in river dance clothes.

"You one of them rodeo school clowns?" asked the first two cowboys I shook hands with.

"No, actually I'm just a visitor, but I'm feeling more clownish by the minute. Do you know a place around here where a guy might buy himself a hat, or some boots, or, say, maybe a pistol to shoot himself?"

I did not really say any of these things, because it was easier just to nod and lie about being one of the rodeo clowns. By the time we finished our first Bible study and headed for the ring the following morning, I was still hatless and bootless, and pretty much resigned to looking like Harpo Marx.

"I thought we might start you out pulling chutes," said Lyle, all perky-like. "That way you can see it up close and personal—you know, learn the gate procedures, find out what a rodeo cowboy does for a living. By the way, nice high-tops."

"Thanks, Lyle."

The experience was immediately addicting. My job was to stand inside the ring, grasping a rope that led to the chute gate. On the other side of the gate was two tons of attitude, topped with a hundred and thirty pounds of trembling cow-*wanna*-boy.

When the boy gave the nod, I gave a tug and got out of the way really fast.

Bull after bull, the gate procedures were exactly the same.

The young cow-*wanna*-boy would climb up onto the fence and slowly ease himself down on the bull. With the help of the real cowboys, he would bind his hand to the beast by wrapping his hand with a rope, and then he would scoot forward, centering himself right above the shoulder blades.

When everything was ready, he would mash his cowboy hat down on his head, freeze for what seemed like an eternity, and then finally give the nod. That was my cue to pull the gate, and run like the dickens to avoid getting trampled.

I watched three ambulances come and go that first day, carting off the wounded riders and their wailing girlfriends. All in all, day one was fascinating.

On day two I taught the cowboys about Jesus again, then went to the ring planning on pulling gates. Lyle had other plans for me.

"I thought we might put you on a mechanical bull this morning, so you can see what a cowboy's backside goes through. I think you'll enjoy the ride."

Lyle was right. I did enjoy the ride, and my boys enjoyed watching me enjoy it.

"Daddy rode a mannickle bull today," Peter told his grandma on the phone that night.

"That's nice. Is your daddy okay?" asked grandma.

"No, he fell in some poop."

This was true; I did fall in some poop, but only because Lyle had placed it there to make the experience more realistic for me. I also want to mention that I rode the "mannickle" for sixteen seconds. That night I went to bed next to my wife feeling more like a man than I had felt in a long time. The following morning I felt as if the mannickle had ridden me.

"You up for working the chutes again?" asked Lyle when I saw him at breakfast on day three.

"I'm always up," I said stiffly.

"How'd you like to look more official today?"

"Sure. I guess."

Lyle handed me a cream-colored Stetson, some well-worn chaps, and a pair of boots that fit me perfectly.

"Where'd you get these?" I asked, gathering the gear in my arms.

"You remember that last fella who went to the hospital in the ambulance yesterday—the one who was about your size?"

"What about him?"

"Well, if anyone ever asks him if he has ridden to the hospital in just his Skivvies, he won't have to fib."

Lyle winked at me and walked away; he is one of those guys who you're never quite sure is telling the truth or not. Cindy says the best way to catch Lyle in a lie is to see if his lips are moving.

An hour later I was just minding my business, pulling gates, looking cool in my new duds, dodging death, when Lyle sauntered in my direction.

"The next one's yours," he said casually. Then he started to walk off.

"What do you mean, next one?"

"You know—the next bull we roll through the gates. I think it's a brindle," he added, gazing through the bars at the animal-in-waiting. "He's kinda old, so he probably won't stomp you too bad."

"Whoa, now—"

"'Whoa' don't work with a critter this big, pardner. You may as well drop it from your vocabulary."

"But you promised I wouldn't be getting on any animals."

"I've been kicked in the head a few times. Sometimes I don't mean to say the things I do."

I never learned the bull's name, but in the middle of all the hubbub of me climbing trancelike up the fence, and easing timidly onto an animal the size of a Buick, and packing my hand, and mashing my hat, and cursing Lyle, someone with good intentions suggested that if I lived through the experience, I ought to rent a video entitled *My Heroes Have Always Been Cowboys*. Apparently my bull, or a much younger and meaner version of him, stars in the opening scenes. I still haven't rented it.

"Stay in the middle," said Lyle.

"I have no idea what you're talking about," I replied.

I gave the nod, and my life became a blur.

Born in California.

Raised an Okie.

Surrounded by three sisters.

Avoided estrogen poisoning by constantly proving I was not a girl.

Basketball.

Football.

Tennis.

Weights.

Rock climbing.

Cliff diving.

Bull riding.

Bull?

★ ★ ★

Wham! I hit the ground. Up I jumped from the poop and the mud, scrambling for the fence like a cockroach for the cupboard.

"Yee-haw, city slicker!" cried Lyle from the announcer's box. "You done rode that bull for seven seconds."

"Is that good?" I asked, safe now behind the fence. My bull had lost interest in me and was meandering in the direction of some attractive heifers on the other side of the holding pen.

"That'll do," said Lyle.

My sons clapped loudly and told me I was a hero. Cindy eyed me like those heifers were eyeing my bull—turning up her nose at my manure-spattered getup with a strange mix of revulsion and attraction.

A day or two later someone explained to me that my ride had come up one second short of the time required for a complete ride. But I didn't care. Cindy said I was seven seconds closer than most men, and that was good enough for her. She kept that heifer look in her eyes for a couple of weeks—until I forgot to take out the trash, or drank out of the milk carton, or something. Then I went from being Marlboro Man to Pasty White City Guy pretty quickly.

I need to ride bulls more often.

A man who loses his temper doesn't plan on it. He is like a cowboy who falls off his horse and lands on his head. It just happens.

So how does one get prepared? How does one *plan* to win a family fight?

I will tell you.

It begins in the chute—in the last calm moments before the gate swings open, and you have to start your day. Maybe your chute is a chair in your bedroom, or a porch swing with a view of your backyard. I personally do a lot of thinking in the shower. Sometimes I get down on my knees and raise my hands to the ceiling and say something like, "God, here is the best I have to offer You today—my pitiful, naked self. If You have any plans for doing something through me today, I apologize ahead of time for the working conditions. As I have said, this is the best I have to offer. Amen."

I know this is weird. But the fact is—*I'm* weird. And the concept of God living inside a weirdo like me is also weird. Nevertheless, it's true. He knows what I'm about to face in a few moments, when the gate flies open and I have to begin my day. He loves me, and he loves the people who love me, too. He wants to wash my heart clean every morning, so that I might approach all my relationships with the same fresh outlook. But this process doesn't just happen by itself. I must join God in the gate procedures. I must climb up on the fence, straddle the bull, mash my hat down on my head, and pack my own hand. God "cowboys up" for no one. Men and women must prepare themselves for the fights ahead, and when it's all said and done...they must give the nod.

Preparing for a fight begins with the same simple question every morning: *Do I really love God today?* My answer to this question determines what today's fights will be like. If I say, "Yes, I do love God," then my next question ought to be, "How do I intend to show this love to my family? To my neighbors? To the world?"

Family fights are often like wild, unpredictable bulls. Too many people approach these bulls like uppity schnauzers—arrogant, unknowledgeable of the gate procedures, nipping at the heels of their opponent, and getting kicked in the chops for their efforts. But the prepared and confident cowboy rides the bull every time.

Let me tell you my secret for starting a good fight:

Live each day as if you are in a pasture, but prepare for each day as if you are in a pen.

In other words, get your heart ready.

Because you never know when the chutes are going to open, and the next bull through the gate will be "yours."

Cooking with Bat Dung

CHECKMATE

**Anyone can start a fight.
It's the finishing that's tricky.**

Getting old is tough. People who disagree probably haven't started losing games to their kids yet.

I'm not talking about the occasional "thrown" game of Candy Land, or the obligatory, photo-finish footrace to the van after church—

> "They're neck and neck, coming around the corner! Now Wesley surges ahead on the homestretch, and is countered by Dad with his own burst of speed! But what's this? It looks like trouble for Dad; he seems to have thrown a loafer and is struggling just to keep up. It's Wesley by a nose. It's Wesley by two noses. It's…it's…it's a tie! Where, oh where did Will Cunningham summon the courage to make that final push toward the tape?"

"Dad?"
"Yup?"
"How come we always tie?"
"Because neither of us is a loser, son."

If you're over forty, you know that losing happens eventually. The first loss is the hardest. Mine was a game of H-O-R-S-E to Wes, and I was so stunned I instantly became a compulsive gambler.

"I'll play you again for a dollar," I said.

"I don't want to take your money, Dad."

"You worry about your game, and I'll worry about my money."

"All right—but you're going to be sorry."

"Sorry, my...foot. Just shoot the ball."

He beat me soundly and I subpoenaed for an immediate double-or-nothing rematch, thinking sooner or later my luck would heat up or his skills would cool down. Neither happened, and ten games later I owed Wes five hundred and twelve dollars. He tried to act casual about it, but inside his heart I knew he was cutting down the nets and running around the court like Jim Valvano. In the course of an hour I had gone from "Dad the Supreme Despot" to "Dad the Decrepit Slot Machine Addict." To Wesley's credit, he attempted to comfort me—but I was beyond help.

"You don't have to pay me, you know," said Wesley.

"Yeah, right—and I suppose I don't have to show you that a man's word is the most valuable thing he owns, either. No thanks."

Suddenly an idea came to me that was both face-saving and fiscally sound.

"How about if we go double or nothing again?" I said.

"What—and lose your house and cars?"

"Very funny, Wes. If you're scared, just admit it."

Wes looked at me out of the corner of his eye, and for a moment I was certain I saw a flicker of understanding.

"I'll shoot first," he said with a smile.

Chess is another example of the getting-old thing. I thought at least I could hang on to my crown until my boys were out of high school. But not long after the H-O-R-S-E debacle, my chess dynasty also went down in flames, and I took to shuffling around the house in my bathrobe.

No other game ends quite so abruptly and regally as chess. It is a marvelous game, a royal one even; and it formed the basis for Cindy's and my favorite chapter in the first edition of *Family Fight*.

We had wondered for a long time how to end a fight. It should come naturally, we thought, like the logical progression of *A* plus *B* equals *C*.

But that was never the case for us. We could follow all the rules of a wholesome fight—sticking to the present issues, avoiding unnecessary roughness, speaking heartfelt "I'm sorry's" and "I forgive you's"; and yet when it was all said and done, we could still feel as comfortable as a rash around each other.

How does one end one of these? we wondered. *How do two people who have just gone toe-to-toe over something start enjoying their marriage again?*

We desperately wanted to know.

As I've said already, chess provided the key. Something about that final pronouncement of "Checkmate!" got us to thinking. And then, of course, you know where thinking always leads.

To trouble.

★ ★ ★

We were in seminary when it became clear for us. Seminaries are great for making discoveries. Maybe this is because they tend to be places where old guys go to ponder the nature of things. And with all that pondering going on, like a giant magnifying glass bringing light to bear on a piece of notebook paper, reducing the sun to a nickel-size inferno—there is bound to be some fiery revelations.

Ours flared up one night just before the Thanksgiving break.

We were living in a small apartment near the campus that semester. We loved our little place and Cindy did a wonderful job of decorating it, but over the months, we had become increasingly aware of how cramped it was.

For instance, my desk, where I did most of my studying, was right in the middle of our living room—not the most academic atmosphere. And on this particular evening I was up late working on a theology paper.

"Need company?" asked Cindy, just as I seated myself for the long night ahead.

Now if I had stopped right there and examined the context clues, I would have seen that Cindy's words held deeper meaning. And if I had really applied myself to extracting their meaning, I would have packed up my books, kissed my wife, and trudged through the snow to the seminary library to do my studying. What Cindy *really* meant when she asked if I wanted company was, "I'd love to talk, and I'd prefer you weren't studying while we did it."

But I am a troglodyte, with stumps on the sides of my head for ears; and so I plunged ahead with my theology paper, allowing Cindy to settle on the sofa next to me. Already she had that glazed look in her eyes one gets after a delicious hour spent reading *Southern Living* magazine. I should have seen it, but I was deep in my cave.

Then it happened.

"Honey?" Cindy began. "What kind of bread do you think I should bake for Thanksgiving?"

"Mmmmm...bread...good," I said with primitive enthusiasm.

"Should it be honey wheat or sesame seed?"

"Honey wheat...good."

"Or maybe I could make potato bread. I don't know. What kind do you want, Will?"

I looked up from my paper and realized we were speaking English to one another, and that I was not in fact sitting in a cave with saber-toothed tiger bones and systematic theology books piled up around me.

"Are you asking me something?" I said stupidly.

"Will! We've been having a conversation for ten minutes!"

"We have?"

"Yes!"

"Okay—tell me the part I missed."

"Well, I was telling you about the trouble I was having deciding what kind of bread to make for Thanksgiving...and with the holiday just around the corner...and potato bread being all the rage right now...and with it being so hard to make...and so honey wheat might be the best bet...and that's why I thought...and maybe sesame seed is an option...and then...and just...and bread...and...and...and..."

Pretty soon I was back in my cave, tinkering around with redaction criticism, and general revelation, and why in the world bats thought it was their right to fly into my living room and relieve themselves, when all of a sudden I heard a familiar voice coming to me through the swamp gas.

"I haven't made sourdough in a long time. How about sourdough?"

This time I looked up at Cindy, to show her I had heard every word she said.

"Honey wheat's fine," I replied.

Cindy's mouth dropped open like a codfish's.

"We weren't talking about honey wheat, Will. We were talking about sourdough."

"Sourdough's fine, too."

I quickly dropped my eyes, hoping Cindy would catch the message. *Please, God. Make Cindy go to bed*, I thought.

Apparently, God didn't hear me, because no sooner had I settled down in my cave again than I heard Cindy launching into a discourse on the rigors of baking with high-altitude flour.

And I lost it.

"Cindy," I said, with all the couth of a man who cooks his food over bat dung, "make honey wheat bread! Make sesame seed bread! Make potato bread, or sourdough bread, or sour potato honey seed bread! But whatever kind of bread you make, do it quietly!"

For a moment Cindy looked as if she had been hit in the face with a club. Then the tears came. Followed by the very thing I had been trying to avoid—two hours of discussion and apologies and more discussion, and, needless to say, no studying. Finally we resolved the matter, but we both still felt lousy.

Then Cindy did an amazing thing. She got up from the sofa and went into the kitchen. Soon she was back, and in her hands was a small bowl filled with my favorite snack—potato chips. She gave me a kiss on the cheek and went to bed.

Checkmate!

The game was over, and surprisingly it felt like we were both winners.

Do you see the principle? Checkmate means simply this: When you've done all you can to resolve conflict yet still feel lousy, go back and *check your mate*. In other words, don't just leave him or her high and dry. Check to see how he or she is feeling, and then—and here's the crucial part—accompany this check with an act of love.

When all the words have been said, don't say any more words; an act of sacrificial love is the necessary, final move to bring about resolution. It's the bowl of potato chips that says, "Truce." It's the back rub that says, "Everything's okay." It's the last move on the board that says, "Checkmate...I love you."

This is the secret to ending a fight and getting back to normal. *Checkmate.* It will change the way you end your fights forever.

Oh, yeah. Hundreds of H-O-R-S-E games later, I think I owe Wes roughly the equivalent of the national debt.

But who's counting?

BREAKFAST BY THE SEA

"Checkmate."

"Uncle!"

"Truce!"

A white flag waving.

Three slaps on the mat.

A mushroom cloud over Hiroshima.

Pulling out of Nam.

A divorce.

A breakfast by the sea.

There are dozens of ways to end a fight. But really...a breakfast by the sea?

Have you ever offended someone, and then longed to win back his or her friendship? That period between the rift and the reunion is a desperate time. Waiting. Wondering. "Does she still love me?" "Does he still want me around?" You know the feeling. Peter, that impulsive, loudmouthed disciple of Jesus, knew it, too.

If words could kill, then Peter committed suicide a thousand times. His tongue was his downfall, and on one occasion he found himself at war with the Son of God. Caught in the throes of an angry mob, Jesus was led away to be tried and sentenced for His claims of deity. All but one of his friends deserted him. Peter followed at a safe distance. The mob marched on, through the courtyard gates and into the gaping jaws of the Praetorian Guard. The doors slammed. Peter hid in the shadows and wondered, *What will I say if I'm discovered?*

Soon enough he knew: "I don't even know him!"

Peter spoke these five short words three separate times. And less than a day later, Jesus was dead on a cross. Three days later, some women went to mourn for Jesus at His gravesite but found an empty tomb.

An angel greeted them with these words: "Go, tell His disciples and Peter, 'He is going before you into Galilee; there you will see Him, just as He said to you.'"

I think that message was meant mostly for Peter. Note how he is singled out from the rest of the disciples. I can imagine Jesus dictating to that angel and making him repeat himself until he had it down just right, especially the part about Peter. "Make sure that *Peter* knows I'm alive."

I wonder how Peter felt when he heard the news. Elated? Maybe. Relieved? Perhaps. But I think he also felt a little like the outlaw who ambushes Clint Eastwood and doesn't quite finish the job. It's terrible not knowing where you stand with someone you've offended.

"What will He think of me now?" Peter probably asked himself as he prepared his fishing nets. His three years with Jesus seemed only a dream to him now, a blurred glimpse into the world of miracles and prophecies and spirits.

Now he was back where he belonged—he could mend nets and sails, and forget about mending blind men and beggars. Here he could fish for fish, and forget about fishing for men's souls.

One morning, after fishing all night and catching nothing, Peter spotted a thin line of smoke rising from the beach nearby.

Thoughts

A man stooped over his fire and tended the breakfast that sizzled over it. The aroma drifted over the waves until it reached the boat full of hungry men, enticing them toward the shore.

"Any fish, boys?" the man shouted.

It was a familiar voice. Peter had heard it before. They all had. "No," replied the men. "We've caught nothing."

"Then throw your net on the right side and you'll get plenty of them," said the man.

With reluctance, the veteran fishermen obeyed the voice from the shore, for it sounded like a command. And anyway—they had nothing to lose.

Soon they hauled so many fish into the boat that there was barely room for the men. By now, everyone knew exactly who the man on the beach was. It was the Lord!

While they were still far off, Peter, in his excitement, leaped into the sea and swam toward the beach. As he swam he must have been thinking, *What will I say to him? What will I do?*

Intellectually, Peter knew that he was forgiven. After all, the Jesus he had lived with for three years was in the habit of forgiving people. But emotionally, Peter still felt cut off from the Lord. By the time he reached land he knew what he would do. He would busy himself with the catch of the day. And he did just that.

Picture Peter as he tries to avoid his friend, Jesus, whom he denied just a short time before. Head down, hands moving fast, overdramatizing his involvement with some knot, Peter is too busy to make eye contact as he single-handedly tallies the fish—"One hundred and fifty one…one hundred and fifty two…one

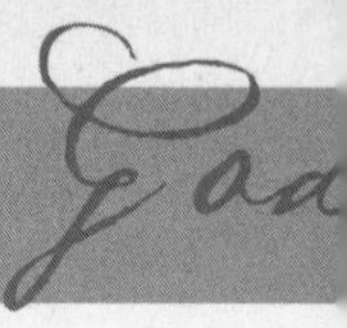

hundred and fifty three…" Meanwhile, his friends are laughing and eating a fine fish breakfast with Jesus.

Finally the job is done and Peter has nothing with which to occupy himself. His hands fidget, so he wipes them on his thighs. The men are quiet now; most of them are knee-deep in the sea, rinsing the grime of their trade from their tired bodies. Behind Peter the fire crackles.

Jesus speaks. "There's fish and bread for you, Peter. Do you want them?"

Peter's eyes fill with tears. His face is still turned toward the sea, his back toward the fire. He is remembering mealtimes with Jesus. There was the wedding feast at Cana when Peter had first joined Jesus and His followers. When Jesus turned the water into wine and saved the groom from embarrassment, Peter knew he was following someone special.

He remembered the supper on the northern slopes of the Galilean sea, just east of Capernaum. That was a marvelous meal. Jesus praying over a handful of food and then feeding five thousand people with it—what a miracle!

Finally, there was that last supper, the one he did not want to remember. At that meal, Jesus had spoken of betrayal, denial, death…and a cock's crow.

The tears begin to flow down Peter's face and collect in his beard. Then he feels a hand on his shoulder, and he hears the words he has longed to hear.

"Come, friend. Your breakfast is almost cold. And by the way—I forgive you."

You would think that Jesus would say something like, "By

the power invested in me, I hereby declare Peter guiltless, forgiven, and reinstated as pillar in the church universal." But he didn't. Instead, Jesus went beyond mere words. And with an ordinary token of service...a few morsels of food...He restored the big fisherman to his sanity and to his Lord.

When was the last time you ended a fight with someone in your family by serving them? Perhaps you feel that your efforts would prove unsuccessful if you tried. Or maybe you believe that you are above that sort of behavior. If that's the case, then remember Christ's example.

There was once a lonely fisherman, his life a shambles, his faith a wreck. So God gathered wood, squatted on a beach, lit a fire, and cooked him breakfast by the sea.

Checkmate.

Pass the fish.

Current Affairs

THE TRAGEDY OF LUST AND ANGER

I saw my first dirty photograph when I was eight and, try as I might to remove it, the image is still fastened firmly to the refrigerator door of my brain.

I want to talk to just the men here, but I don't know what to say to make the women go away. It seems rude to invite someone to a party and then ask them to leave—particularly an entire gender.

Are they gone yet?

Someone take a peek to see if there are any stragglers with their ears to the door.

No? Good.

Now, to our topic: What would you do if you discovered your wife was having an affair?

Don't answer too quickly; think about it—really force yourself to think about it.

Assume that your wife and her lover didn't develop their relationship overnight; it grew over a period of years, even decades. They met before you ever knew her, on a lonely street corner…or in an airport…or at a motel, during one of her first business trips. She was vulnerable; he was charming. Almost immediately their souls were soldered together.

At first she did her best to resist him, and when the two of you became involved, you became her convenient excuse. She threw herself into you, as wholeheartedly as possible, but in the back of her mind he was always nearby. Soon you were married, and your wife thought your constant companionship would make her forget about her lover. But she was wrong.

Over time you got busy with your job and had less time to work out, so your once firm physique lost a battle with gravity. On the other hand, Lover Boy was independently wealthy and had all the time in the world to maintain his body. He was looking good—and your wife was looking *at him* more than ever.

Time passed, and with it came the kids and pets. Besides the energy these required, there was also the lawn, the garden, and the cottage at the lake. Your times with your wife grew fewer and further between. Strangely, she didn't seem to mind; she was far down the track in her extramarital relationship, and there were no signs of the train slowing down.

Everything seemed different now about your wife—her reactions to the kids, her response to you in bed, even the way she related to God. You can't remember the last time you heard your wife pray. In fact, you can't remember your wife at all.

It seems she left home forever ago.

Men, this is not an easy read, is it? When I was planning this chapter and talking it through with Cindy, I almost decided not to write it. Of course you recognize I'm not talking about a real affair, as is evidenced by the fact I purposely withheld a face, a name, and most other human traits. Your wife's lover is pornography, and he is composed of pixels and paper. Truth is, your wife is not very interested in such a lover—most women aren't.

So let's return to reality.

Pornography is an affair of the heart, carried on almost exclusively by men. Certainly women are connected to it, or there would not be any pornography; and, yes, there is a small population of women who seek it for pleasure. But the overwhelming majority of women hate it in all its forms.

Every year I am part of a team that travels for twelve weeks interviewing college athletes from Stanford to Savannah, from Ole Miss to the mountains of Colorado, and most points in between. We are interviewing these students to come to Kanakuk, where they will pour out their lives in a demonstration of the living Christ.

At all costs we must have men and women whose minds are pure.

Without exception, when an interviewee and I arrive at the question on the application form that addresses past or present use of pornography, there is always a pause.

Men pause shamefully. Even the strong, spiritual types who have dabbled in porn cannot bring themselves to look at me. They always look down and to the left, as if the image they are remembering is as near as their hand.

Women, on the other hand, pause disgustedly, as if they can't believe we have to discuss the topic of pornography in an interview for a Christian sports camp. In my nine years of service at Kanakuk, I have looked at least a thousand college women in the eyes and asked the same question: "What do you think of pornography?" It should not surprise you that *every single one* of them said they loathed it and did not engage in it.

Men, please understand that women hate pornography.

When we bring it into our eyes, our ears, our hearts, and our homes we are introducing our wives to our lover—the one we met so long ago on that lonely street corner…or at that distant airport…or at that sad, secluded motel. Your lover is destroying your home, bit by bit, brick by brick. It's a slow and steady process, but in the end it will be thorough.

Why does the topic of pornography belong in a book about family fights? To begin with, all conflicts require energy; and proper conflict demands even more of it. It is also true that affairs, be they real or make-believe, require energy, too—a great deal of it. Try keeping one small secret for a while, and you will soon see what I mean. It stands to reason, then, that the man who spends his energy on an affair will have little left to spend on a family fight.

So, what really is an "affair of the heart"? Jesus gives a clear definition in Matthew 5 of His famous Sermon on the Mount, when He says, "You have heard that it was said, 'Do not commit adultery.' But I tell you that anyone who looks at a woman lustfully has already committed adultery with her in his heart."

There is your definition.

But someone may well say, "How does one know if he's in an affair of the heart?" Here is how you can know:

1. If you race to the mailbox to intercept things like women's clothing catalogs and lingerie magazines before your wife can retrieve them, you are in an affair of the heart.
2. If you flip channels mindlessly, particularly after the family has gone to bed, and you find yourself lingering on *any* image that is remotely sensual, you are in an affair of the heart.
3. If you pleasure yourself with any regularity, even though you have a God-given outlet with your wife, you are in an

affair of the heart. (And yes, I did say "pleasure yourself" in this book.)

4. If you listen to or engage in phone sex, you are in an affair of the heart.
5. And finally, if you refuse to filter your Internet and spend an increasing amount of time surfing in the late hours, you are in danger of the fastest growing destroyer of homes on the planet, and you are having an affair of the heart.

Notice how I haven't even mentioned the so-called hard core examples of a make-believe affair—things like *Hustler* magazine, XXX videos, massage shops, and strip joints. As long as men can say they haven't stooped as low as these, they can often fool themselves into thinking they are faithful. But give me ten honest men, and I'll show you seven who are liars.

The man who is at his best is the man who admits his worst; this is the man God employs in His kingdom. This is the growing body of men who are winning family fights.

So, what can you do to break the power of an affair and leave it behind? Here are eight things that will help you:

1. **Confess (James 5:16).** Find someone you trust, and tell him everything. Then go with that man and tell your wife. Chances are she has "known" for a long time.
2. **Say yes (James 4:7–8).** Too much emphasis has been put on saying no to temptation; this leaves men feeling empty and defeated. Saying no to temptation is a vital part of purity, but only if it is accompanied by saying yes to new

and holy things that can replace the old, sensual ones. The James 4 passage and others like it that contain a promise have, over the years, become my way of holding God to His part of the deal. Just like the Israelites with their backs to the Red Sea, God wants us to "stand still" and see what He will do for us in troubled times. Besides memorizing and standing on such passages, I recommend some very practical things, like…

3. **Rest.**
4. **Exercise regularly.**
5. **Spend time with friends, play sports, and make memories.**
6. **Shut all old windows to filth** and open new ones to truth (e.g., Christian radio, music, and literature).
7. **Serve someone.** There is nothing like serving someone else to make for a healthier "you." This includes everything from dating your wife to shoveling snow off your neighbor's driveway.
8. **And finally, enjoy sex with your wife.** God gave her to you for enjoyment. Cultivate the joy.

All right, men—what I have told you in this chapter is true and tested. I have battled with these things like many of you, and have had both successes and failures. But the good news is the failures are fewer and smaller, and it is not because my appetite for sex has decreased; it is because my love for Jesus has *increased.* It does me good to draw near Him, and to remember that He is familiar with all my temptations. He helps me face my afflictions one day at a time—and because of Him my home is much happier.

End the affairs today, men. "If your right hand is causing you to sin, cut it off. If your right eye is causing you to sin, gouge it out." These words of Jesus are not a mandate for masochism; they are a recommendation for volitional limits based on the seriousness of sexual sin. They are the first-century equivalent of saying, "If your high-speed Internet access causes you to look at porn, yank the plug out of the wall!"

Once again, end the affairs today—then do it again tomorrow, and the next day, and the next, until finally you are free of the attraction that nearly proved fatal. Soon, you'll discover you have more energy when a family fight arises; and you'll find these fights more pleasant and manageable.

I am praying for your freedom, brothers.

Feel free to pray for mine.

Why We Fuss

**I think if people fought with broccoli
strapped to their foreheads,
fights would be a lot shorter...and funnier.**

I am traveling with a black man as I write this chapter. We are on a business trip in a state just northeast of the Bible belt. It is a lovely place with trees so multicolored that one would assume its residents are just as happily integrated. But this would be a wrong assumption.

Being with Antoine for many miles has allowed me to see things through his eyes—such as the look on his face when the waiter at the Italian restaurant makes a racist comment, then follows it up by writing "Thank you, please come again" on everyone's receipt *except* Antoine's. It is as if he doesn't exist—as if a ghost ate the lasagna on his plate.

Earlier this morning we were interviewing college students in one of those Norman Rockwell towns: malt shops, tree-canopied streets, jack-o'-lanterns on porches, Notre Dame beating the crud out of someone on the radio. We asked a man about the history of the town, and he told us about a founding father who gave a great sum of money for the city hall to be built, and then wrote into the bylaws that if a black family ever moved to town, the city hall had to be demolished.

Today, a hundred years later, there are black families in that town, and its city hall still stands. Nevertheless, there remains a disparity in the way its citizens speak to Antoine and me as we pass them on the sidewalk.

"Hail, fellow white man! How is Your Whiteness today?" they greet me warmly.

But not a word is said to Antoine. He passes by like a ghost.

Unrecognized.

Unwelcome.

Undone by the wrecking ball of indifference.

I want to talk to you in these closing pages about the source of conflict. This may seem like a point that should have been made at the beginning of the book. But I want you to know that sources or origins are about more than just the beginnings of things. They are also the important underpinnings of one's entire life, and are usually close at hand in some fashion when a person finally dies.

This is why I think it is good for a person to return to certain sources, certain roots now and then—like revisiting the neighborhood one grew up in, or hiking to the alpine trickle that spawns a mighty river, or rewriting a twenty-year-old manuscript because it may still have something to say.

The source of conflict is a wicked one—steadfast and stubborn like the weeds you have tried to rid your garden of. No matter how many times you pluck them, the roots evade you, and your garden looks like gutter trash. The source of conflict is *my desire to have what you have.* It has always been that way. Adam and Eve wanted much more than an apple; they wanted God's throne, His authority, and His right to decide the menu in the restaurant.

"What do you mean, 'apples are seasonal'? We want an apple now! And by golly, we're going to have one!"

They got their apple, all right—and the terrible conflict that followed.

Pride is another word for all of this. It is the best explanation for the foolishness Antoine endures in so many hamlets across our nation. Pride says, "My ways and my wants are more important than your ways and your wants," or "My whiteness is more important than your blackness." Pride is the taproot of conflict and the reason the weeds of bad fighting lurch across our republic, choking the homes between its shores.

Pride leads to fear.

Not only do I want my way, but I am also afraid you are going to keep me from getting it. This makes you my enemy, and so I fight with you.

Pride also leads to curse.

Genesis 3 goes a long way in explaining why men and women fight so poorly today. Here we catch a glimpse of the fall of mankind. The separation of creation from Creator, the discovery of emotional and physical nakedness, the plunge into interrelational darkness—these were just a few of the consequences of Adam and Eve's rebellion. The word *curse* is used throughout Genesis 3, describing a reality that reaches into all aspects of life, then and now, including the way people conflict with one another.

Listen to what God said to the man and the woman after their disobedience:

To the woman He said,

> "I will greatly multiply your pain in childbirth,
> In pain you shall bring forth children;
> Yet your desire will be for your husband,
> And he will rule over you."

Then to Adam He said, "Because you have listened to the voice of your wife, and have eaten from the tree about which I commanded you, saying, 'You shall not eat from it';

> Cursed is the ground because of you;
> In toil you will eat of it all the days of your life.
> Both thorns and thistles it shall grow for you;
> And you will eat the plants of the field;
> By the sweat of your face
> You will eat bread,
> Till you return to the ground,
> Because from it you were taken;
> For you are dust,
> And to dust you shall return."
> (Genesis 3:16–19, NASB)

After witnessing the birth of our son Wesley, I recognize one of the inevitable elements of God's curse upon the woman. It just plain hurts to have a baby, as Cindy will quickly tell you.

But some aspects of the curse in Genesis 3 may still puzzle you. For instance, why would it be a curse for a woman's desire to be for her husband, as verse 16 implies? From a husband's point of view, that sounds like a bargain. However, when we link that portion of verse 16 with the verse's last phrase, the curse comes into plain view.

"And he shall rule over you."

Here is a woman with an intense desire for her husband to love her. Some Old Testament commentaries describe this desire as bordering on disease (the Hebrew word translated here as "desire" stems from a word which means "to have a violent craving for a person or thing"). But the woman's desire is not satisfied. Instead of meeting her needs, her husband often withholds his love from her. In short, he holds a position of rulership over his wife.

I don't believe God's original intent in creating Adam and Eve was for one of them to rule over the other. That was a direct result of disobedience. Certainly there are functional roles in a family that require men to lead, but that's a different matter for a different book. What I am trying to say here is that having Adam rule over her is the crowning blow of Eve's curse. Whereas the man and the woman once had perfect fellowship, now they have alienation and conflict. Their relationship, initially characterized in terms of oneness and suitability, now is described in terms of domination and unmet desire.

Put yourself in Eve's position. Imagine that you have an intense desire for Adam, and a deep longing for your relationship to be as it once was. Yet Adam seems strangely distant, preoccupied with more important matters, such as his work. You have tried everything you know to get him to respond to you, to come toward you, but he only retreats, calling you a "nag." In essence, he rules over you. He always seems to get his way, and you always seem to lose.

Herein is one of the deepest and saddest roots of marital conflict, and it lies in Eve's curse. It is as if God came to Eve after she sinned and said, "Eve, My dear daughter, you have broken the relationship you once had with Me. You have lost the intimate path to My heart, where you have always been able to find validation for your beauty, your ideas, your giftedness, and your wildest dreams. Now, you will try to find that same validation in a flawed human being, named Adam, and he will let you down time and again, until it nearly drives you crazy. This is your curse, Eve, and your only way out of it is to find your way back to Me."

If, in the old days when I was counseling, you were to join me in my office during a typical marriage counseling session, you would have seen at one end of the couch a woman trying desperately to get her husband to show interest in her and the family. At the other end you would see a man wholly devoted to something else—usually his job. You might almost see the frustration oozing from his furrowed brow. With arms crossed, he complains that his wife and kids never appreciate anything he does and that they constantly place new demands on his time. In truth he is a modern-day Adam sweating out his curse.

"I work hard, and look what I get!" says the man. He wants fruit, but his reward is thistles. He views his wife as a nag, not as his friend anymore.

But how else can she gain the attention of a man who is always at work, toiling under the curse of his labor?

By now you can see that this curse is a big reason men and women fight so poorly with one another. If you can picture a woman chasing a man who is chasing a job, then you have pretty much summarized the sad state of most relationships. Eve seeks happiness from a flawed human being named Adam—and Adam seeks happiness from an inanimate object known as "job." It's hard to say whose curse is the worst.

Do you want to know how to make the madness end? If

you are a woman, stop loading your man's shoulders with your expectations. You know the ones I'm talking about—the domestic ones, the social ones, the spiritual ones, the financial ones, the emotional ones, the romantic ones, the parental ones, and the mysterious ones that fall under a nameless heading but are somehow supposed to be understood by your man and carried out flawlessly. You know—*those.* Stop it! Stop loading his shoulders; they are not big enough to handle all your expectations—they were never meant to be.

Instead, view your expectations as a Christmas list. Whatever your man places under the tree for you, receive it gladly as a "gift," not a "given." The rest of your list you can give to God, the one who died to make your dreams come true. Quit chasing your man, and start chasing God.

And if you are a man, you are a bigger fool than Eve. No job can ever meet our needs. Jobs aren't real; they don't have a beating heart beneath a warm breast. What are we thinking, brothers? Do we really believe we can cuddle up to an armful of thistles and find satisfaction? Jobs come and go. Money comes and goes. But our God waits quietly for us to return to Him. He took a crown of thorns on His head, so we wouldn't have to keep wrestling with thorns here on earth. Work is not evil until we enthrone it and make it our god—then it is diabolical.

When a woman stops chasing her man, and a man stops chasing his job, and both of them journey upward to the throne of God—it is amazing how close the two of them can feel to each other, kneeling there in His presence. It is better than a romantic dinner at her favorite restaurant, better than a promotion from the boss, better than all the sex in the world.

It is love as it was meant to be.

★ ★ ★

James, the half-brother of Jesus, once said, "What is the source of quarrels and conflicts among you? Is not the source your pleasures that wage war in your members? You lust and do not have; so you commit murder. You are envious and cannot obtain; so you fight and quarrel" (James 4:1–2, NASB).

Pride.

Fear.

Envy.

Lust.

No nation can be truly integrated until these cursed weeds are gone. No family can win a family fight until it pulls the weeds—roots and all.

If I could change one thing about my twenty-three years of marriage, I would erase all those times I treated Cindy like a ghost. It follows, then, that I have treated God as a ghost, as well.

This double confession is almost too painful for me to bear. I am worse than the founding fathers of all the nearsighted, black-hating nations of the world. I am the Hitler of the universe, goading my God and my girl into the gas chamber of my pride. I deserve a trial, I know. But I ask the Lord's mercy and the reader's understanding.

Someday I will get it right. Even now, a quarter of a century after Bee Creek Bridge, Cindy is becoming more material to me, more substantial, more…real. Or maybe it is I becoming less of a ghost. Maybe all along we have both been like ghosts transforming into the people God meant us to be.

It's complicated and confusing.

Here is one thing I'm sure of: The pain of Bee Creek Bridge and all the pains Cindy and I have endured since then have made us more authentic, more human. Ghosts don't feel pain; humans do. I think this is what James was trying to get at when he wrote that our trials would lead to our "telios"—our perfection. So many good and perfect things came out of the car wreck.

More than we can count.

A man named Klein pulled us out of the Honda; he became a Christian right there on the spot, and went home and told his unbelieving wife and eleven-year-old daughter. And they became Christians, too. We named our first son after that man. Wesley *Klein* Cunningham will always be a reminder that *gain* comes out of *pain.*

The truck driver who ran into us became a Christian, too. He was seventy-six years old when he plowed head-on into our Honda. He hated Jesus before he went into the hospital; and when he came out Jesus was his Lord.

Our surgeon was an admitted atheist. He told the best jokes—most of them dirty as sin. But we loved him, and our hearts were touched when, in the midst of his busy medical practice, he came all the way to another state to attend our wedding. Ten years after our car wreck, our surgeon's son was killed on the exact same stretch of highway. His death gave us cause to stop by our surgeon's house with a pie, and a hug, and a wordless reminder that God still loved him.

A river of gain flowed out of our car wreck, and it has not stopped watering people since 1981. I think your family fights are like our wreck; they seem so frightening to you at first, but after a while you see that they are leading you closer together, molding you into more of a team.

★ ★ ★

We are fighting more as a team now, Cindy and I—more like players who love each other instead of suspect each other. Our fights are shorter, softer, fewer and further between. We seem to be gaining ground as a team does that is moving down the field. Occasionally we lose yardage, but only occasionally.

Up ahead is the goal line, bright and eternal. I have no idea how far away it is; neither does Cindy. No one seems to know. It could be decades away, or as near as our next car wreck. One thing is certain: We are holding hands in the huddle more often.

I can hardly wait to burst into heaven someday, like a fullback through a wall of would-be tacklers—fingers all broken and taped up, spit flying from my mouthpiece. I will fall face-first on the fresh turf of the celestial city, too tired to do a celebration dance and too happy to care.

I am home at last, and the fight is over.

Suddenly I hear music, vaguely at first, as though through the ear holes of a football helmet, then gradually brighter and clearer, as if a marching band is passing by.

DA-DA-DA!!

DA-DA-DA!!

They are playing the ESPN song.

"Stand up, son," booms a familiar voice behind me. I know that voice. It was with me all those dreary days after Bee Creek. With me through the morphine. With me through the loss of athleticism, and the loss of sensation in my left side. With me through the months of rehabilitation. It is a shockingly clear voice, like the sound of a piano being played on top of Mount Everest.

"Stand up!" the voice booms again. This time I turn to see the Lord.

"You look wonderful," He declares. "A little worse for the wear, but nonetheless wonderful. Come here, son. Let's have that hug we've both been waiting for."

I jump to my feet, feeling lighter than—air? Is that what I just inhaled into my lungs just now? It is more like. . .candy. Breathable candy. A few quick steps, and I am in my Savior's arms.

"Welcome home, My boy," He says.

Over His shoulder, I can see clearly for miles—not in the sense that one sees clearly on earth, with images in the distance appearing purplish and hazy and in need of the brain to fill in the details. But here in heaven I can see with the eyes of an eagle, every facet of every diamond on every petal of every flower for as far as my eyes can see. And now I begin to see people.

I see Cindy first. It does not matter that I preceded her in death, or she me; the fact is, I can no longer remember our deaths, or who died first. I have been living here forever it seems, and at the same time everything is as new as my next breath of candy.

"Run to her, Will," says Jesus. "I think you'll enjoy running here in heaven. You'll find you're a bit faster than you used to be on earth, or I am not the Lord of understatement."

I take a step or two, and when I discover my legs aren't as wobbly as I expect them to be, I blast off across the field like a comet. My God, I am fast! I am so fast I almost streak by Cindy, but she catches me and kisses me in a way I always believed our kisses could have been on earth, had my motives been less ulterior. Somehow sex and romance always got a bit tangled up for me, like an impossible, erotic granny knot.

"Wow!" I exclaim, when Cindy is done kissing me. "What was *that?*"

"That was 'hello.'"

"Are hellos legal here?"

"If they're not, they should be."

"We're not breaking any rules, are we?"

"Do you still love me, Will?"

"Of course I do."

"Then we're bound by our love; just as we are bound by our love to everyone."

I glance at her finger. "But not by marriage?"

"No, dear, not in heaven."

I think about that for a moment, looking down at my own ring-free hand, imagining Cindy saying "hello" to other men besides me. It is a new thought to me, one I will have to get used to, though I have always suspected the absence of jealousy and insecurity in heaven would make a lot of things easier.

"They asked for my ring and my watch at the gate; they said I wouldn't need them anymore."

"Oh, yes—that's for road repairs. They take gold and other inferior materials, and melt them down to plug potholes. Everyone who shows up in heaven makes an opening-day contribution. It's like a toll, if you think about it. You only have to pay it once, though."

"Can we say 'hello' again?" I ask.

Cindy laughs. "We can say hello as long as we want. But remember, I love everyone the same."

She kisses me once more, and the funny thing is I don't feel as if I have to go to second or third base—I am already standing at home plate. I am home! God, I love the sound of it.

"You were a great wife."

"Thanks. You weren't so bad yourself."

"No, really," I say, taking Cindy softly by the chin, and turning her face toward mine. "You were the best."

Cindy blushes. "Thanks. Are you ready to see some other people?"

"Oh, yeah."

"Then take a look over there."

At the far fencepost of a vast field our sons come into view, and I ask Cindy when they died. She just laughs at me again.

"There is no *when* in heaven, honey—only *now.* Wes and Pete could have died yesterday or fifty years from now, and it would all be just the same. We're on the outside of time, above it maybe, I'm not sure, it's all a little hard to explain. We're like people at a train station, waiting for the last trainload of relatives to arrive. Everything about the station, every smell, every friendship, every delightful morsel of food has always been here, and *will always* be here. Only the people still on the train care about the time."

Cindy's mention of food reminds me I haven't eaten since right before my funeral. I am eyeing a bushel of apples when I am bowled over by my boys, and the "hellos" begin all over again. They are a different kind of "hello," mind you, though no less warm and welcoming. Wes puts his arm around me.

"Have you eaten since you arrived, Dad?"

"I was just wondering when someone would ask me that."

"Dad, they've got this great little place around the corner called the Cloud Café; it serves the best eggs in all the universe."

I glance at Wes incredulously.

"Did you say *eggs?"*

"Yeah, why do you ask?"

"I thought you didn't like eggs."

"Didn't like eggs? What makes you say that?"

"You know."

"Know what?"

"Don't tell me you don't know."

"How can I know if you're not making any sense?"

"That time I made you sit in the dark, with your plate full

of scrambled eggs; does that ring a bell? You know, and the lights were out, and your brother had been in bed for almost an hour already, and you were crying, and…"

"Dad?"

"What?"

"What are you talking about?"

"What am I *talking* about? I'll tell you what I'm talking about. I'm talking about that time…"

Suddenly my mind goes blank, at least that part of my mind that used to hold all my old thoughts from earth. It's as if a hatch has been opened up in the back of my head, and a sack or two of the garbage has been dumped out. Normally, this would have alarmed me, as is often the case when a middle-aged person forgets a fact to which he has clung forever. But today it feels great.

"What do you say to the four of us going for some breakfast?" I ask, glancing around at my family. "Does everyone have the time?"

Peter punches me in the arm.

"You've got to stop saying that, Dad."

"Sorry. My bad."

Cindy is laughing at me again, because I am such a nimrod about the time thing. Not that I was ever really great with time anyway. I have the tiniest residual of a memory of being late to my own funeral even, but the memory becomes hazier as I write these words.

At the café, there is a huge line of people spilling out the entrance and onto the surrounding clouds; black people, white people, yellow people, red and brown people. Nobody is in a bad mood about the line, because everyone just wants to chat and get caught up with everyone else. Besides, they know the food is never going to run out.

My buddy Doug is there, wearing his snooty fly-fishing outfit and showing off photos from a recent trout expedition to some faraway planet.

A little ways behind him in the line, I see Danny the lazy-eyed fullback. At first I don't recognize him, but when he finally looks my way I notice his eyes are straight.

"Hey, there!" he says. "Don't I know you from somewhere?"

"Will Cunningham," I reply, extending my hand to shake. "We were Rebels together back on earth."

"That's right! And wasn't there one game when the score kind of got out of control?" Danny taps his forehead with his middle finger. "I've been trying to remember it for some time, but it eludes me."

"Sorry, pal, I don't believe I can help you."

"Oh, well. I'm sure it's not important. Say, have you tried the sno-cones here?"

"I can't say I have."

"I order one *before* every meal, just in case the Rapture comes." Danny pauses for a moment, then smiles at what he has just said.

"See you later, Danny. We've got to go to the back of the line."

As we walk away, Peter nudges me.

"He forgot about the Rapture, Dad."

"Oh, I don't think he really forgot. I just think his brain is new to this heaven thing, sort of like mine."

Farther and farther from the café entrance we go, passing familiar faces and acknowledging them all. Up ahead I see Lisa-Jill, and she smiles at me, which makes me feel so much better about whatever it was that happened back on earth between the two of us. I give her a friendly hug. Fortunately, I get her name right this time, and I see in her eyes that she has forgiven me—

for what I'm not sure, but I suspect it must have been a doozy. Cindy hugs her, too.

On we go, shaking hands, hugging necks, giving the occasional "hello" kiss to this friend and that. Lyle is waiting for his breakfast in full rodeo gear. Behind him are two of the smartly dressed women from the froo-frah shop.

Finally, from way in the back of the line, I see this guy abandon his place and start to run toward me. His hair is darker than I remember it; in fact, it's just nice to see he has hair again. One thing is for sure: He was never that fast when he lived on earth.

With his knees high, and his arms pumping like pistons, he is bearing down on me so fast that I start to get a little concerned about the coming collision. But when he finally reaches me the impact is perfect—just as I'd always hoped it would be. We don't say much for a long, long time. We just hold each other, and pat each other's back, and hardly bother to brush away the warm tears that are rolling down our necks.

Over it all, I hear the sound of angels clapping, and cheering, and hooting and hollering for the saints who have fought the *good fight* and finished the race. In the back of my mind, right next to the hatch where all my shabby earth thoughts have been dumped out into space, is this one last, meager, insignificant bit of knowledge that somehow escaped the trash bin. And it is this:

When one attends any important engagement, be it school, or a wedding, or a graduation, or a date, or a job interview, or a rodeo, or a funeral, or one's acceptance into heaven, it is best if one's attire includes more than just his underwear.

I look down at my pants and I smile.

For once I got something right.